Assessment of Staffing Needs of Systems Specialists in Aviation

Committee on Staffing Needs of Systems Specialists in Aviation

Board on Human-Systems Integration

Division of Behavioral and Social Sciences and Education

NATIONAL RESEARCH COUNCIL
OF THE NATIONAL ACADEMIES

THE NATIONAL ACADEMIES PRESS
Washington, D.C.
www.nap.edu

THE NATIONAL ACADEMIES PRESS 500 Fifth Street, NW Washington, DC 20001

NOTICE: The project that is the subject of this report was approved by the Governing Board of the National Research Council, whose members are drawn from the councils of the National Academy of Sciences, the National Academy of Engineering, and the Institute of Medicine. The members of the committee responsible for the report were chosen for their special competences and with regard for appropriate balance.

This study was supported by Contract No. DTFAWA-12-P-00276 between the National Academy of Sciences and the Federal Aviation Administration of the U.S. Department of Transportation. Any opinions, findings, conclusions, or recommendations expressed in this publication are those of the author(s) and do not necessarily reflect the views of the organizations or agencies that provided support for the project.

International Standard Book Number-13: 978-0-309-28650-3
International Standard Book Number-10: 0-309-28650-6

Additional copies of this report are available from the National Academies Press, 500 Fifth Street, NW, Keck 360, Washington, DC 20001; (800) 624-6242 or (202) 334-3313; http://www.nap.edu.

Printed in the United States of America

Suggested citation: National Research Council. 2013. *Assessment of Staffing Needs of Systems Specialists in Aviation.* Washington, DC: The National Academies Press.

THE NATIONAL ACADEMIES

Advisers to the Nation on Science, Engineering, and Medicine

The **National Academy of Sciences** is a private, nonprofit, self-perpetuating society of distinguished scholars engaged in scientific and engineering research, dedicated to the furtherance of science and technology and to their use for the general welfare. Upon the authority of the charter granted to it by the Congress in 1863, the Academy has a mandate that requires it to advise the federal government on scientific and technical matters. Dr. Ralph J. Cicerone is president of the National Academy of Sciences.

The **National Academy of Engineering** was established in 1964, under the charter of the National Academy of Sciences, as a parallel organization of outstanding engineers. It is autonomous in its administration and in the selection of its members, sharing with the National Academy of Sciences the responsibility for advising the federal government. The National Academy of Engineering also sponsors engineering programs aimed at meeting national needs, encourages education and research, and recognizes the superior achievements of engineers. Dr. C. D. (Dan) Mote, Jr., is president of the National Academy of Engineering.

The **Institute of Medicine** was established in 1970 by the National Academy of Sciences to secure the services of eminent members of appropriate professions in the examination of policy matters pertaining to the health of the public. The Institute acts under the responsibility given to the National Academy of Sciences by its congressional charter to be an adviser to the federal government and, upon its own initiative, to identify issues of medical care, research, and education. Dr. Harvey V. Fineberg is president of the Institute of Medicine.

The **National Research Council** was organized by the National Academy of Sciences in 1916 to associate the broad community of science and technology with the Academy's purposes of furthering knowledge and advising the federal government. Functioning in accordance with general policies determined by the Academy, the Council has become the principal operating agency of both the National Academy of Sciences and the National Academy of Engineering in providing services to the government, the public, and the scientific and engineering communities. The Council is administered jointly by both Academies and the Institute of Medicine. Dr. Ralph J. Cicerone and Dr. C. D. (Dan) Mote, Jr., are chair and vice chair, respectively, of the National Research Council.

www.national-academies.org

COMMITTEE ON STAFFING NEEDS OF SYSTEMS SPECIALISTS IN AVIATION

NANCY T. TIPPINS (*Chair*), Valtera, Corporate Executive Board, Greenville, SC
COLIN G. DRURY, Department of Industrial and Systems Engineering, University of Buffalo, State University of New York
T. MARK HARRISON (NAS), Department of Earth and Space Sciences, University of California, Los Angeles
CHRISTOPHER HART, National Transportation Safety Board, Washington DC
PAUL F. HOGAN, Federal National Security and Emergency Preparedness, The Lewin Group, VA
BRIAN NORMAN, Compass Manpower Experts, LLC, San Antonio, TX
TONYA L. SMITH-JACKSON, Department of Industrial and Systems Engineering, North Carolina A&T State University
WILLIAM J. STRICKLAND, Human Resources Research Organization, Alexandria, VA
ELMORE M. WIGFALL, (Retired) Federal Aviation Administration, Los Angeles, CA

Staff

DANIEL E.J. TALMAGE, JR., Study Director
JEANNE C. RIVARD, Senior Program Officer
ELIZABETH T. CADY, Program Officer

BOARD ON HUMAN-SYSTEMS INTEGRATION

Preface

In January 2012, Congress mandated that the Federal Aviation Administration (FAA) ask the National Research Council (NRC) to review and report back on three areas of the FAA: A staffing model for Airway Transportation Systems Specialists (ATSS), a review of the air traffic controllers model, and a study on NextGen, the FAA's Next Generation Air Transportation System. This first report focuses on ATSS, the FAA employees who maintain and certify the equipment of the National Airspace System (NAS). The report reviews various approaches to establishing staffing levels and the variables that should be incorporated in the development of a model to assist FAA management in correctly establishing staffing levels and allocating the right number of workers to maintain the NAS safely and efficiently.

I wish to express my appreciation to the members of the committee for their diligent and dedicated contributions to the study and to the preparation of this report within an ambitious time frame. The committee's diverse expertise and experience contributed greatly to the broad perspective that is incorporated in this report. The committee is also grateful to the FAA as well as the representatives of the Professional Aviation Safety Specialists for their active participation throughout the study. The committee cannot sufficiently thank the NRC staff members—Barbara Wanchisen, Toby Warden, Jeanne Rivard, Daniel Talmage, Cherie Chauvin, Tina Winters, Elizabeth Cady, and Renée Wilson-Gaines—for their dedication to the study and to the preparation of this report. We would also like to thank Manu Sharma for her administrative support throughout the study process. And finally we thank the executive office reports staff of the Division of Behavioral and Social Sciences and Education, especially Robert Katt (consultant editor), who provided valuable help with editing the report, and Kirsten Sampson Snyder, who managed the report review process. Without the NRC's guidance and wise counsel, the committee's job would have been even more difficult if not impossible.

Nancy T. Tippins, *Chair*
Committee on Staffing Needs
of Systems Specialists in Aviation

Reviewers

This report has been reviewed in draft form by individuals chosen for their diverse perspectives and technical expertise, in accordance with procedures approved by the National Research Council's (NRC's) Report Review Committee. The purpose of this independent review is to provide candid and critical comments that will assist the institution in making its published report as sound as possible and to ensure that the report meets institutional standards for objectivity, evidence, and responsiveness to the study charge. The review comments and draft manuscript remain confidential to protect the integrity of the deliberative process. We wish to thank the following individuals for their review of this report:

Ellen J. Bass, College of Information Science and Technology and College of Nursing and Health Professions, Drexel University
Raymond E. Conley, Manpower, Personnel, and Training Program, RAND Project AIR FORCE, Arlington, VA
Gene T. Crabtree, Jr., (Retired) Technical Operations, Federal Aviation Administration
R. John Hansman (NAE), MIT International Center for Air Transportation, Massachusetts Institute of Technology
Kurt Kraiger, Center for Organizational Excellence, Department of Psychology, Colorado State University
Leif E. Peterson, Advanced HR Concepts & Solutions, LLC, Beavercreek, OH
Karlene H. Roberts, Haas School of Business and Center for Catastrophic Risk Management, University of California, Berkeley
Juan I. Sanchez, Department of Management and International Business, Florida International University
Thomas B. Sheridan (NAE), Departments of Mechanical Engineering and Aeronautics and Astronautics, Massachusetts Institute of Technology (Emeritus)
Philip J. Smith, Department of Industrial and Systems Engineering, The Ohio State University

Although the reviewers listed above have provided many constructive comments and suggestions, they were not asked to endorse the conclusions or recommendations nor did they see the final draft of the report before its release. The review of this report was overseen by the monitor, Wesley L. Harris (NAE), Department of Aeronautics and Astronautics and associate provost, Massachusetts Institute of Technology, and coordinator Jeremiah A. Barondess (IOM), president emeritus and scholar in residence, New York Academy of Medicine. Appointed by the NRC, they were responsible for making certain that an independent examination of this report was carried out in accordance with institutional procedures and that all review comments were carefully considered. Responsibility for the final content of this report rests entirely with the authoring committee and the institution.

Contents

Figures, Tables, and Boxes

FIGURES

TABLES

BOXES

Acronyms and Abbreviations

ADS-B	Automatic Dependent Surveillance-Broadcast
AFL-CIO	American Federation of Labor-Congress of Industrial Organizations
AFMS	Air Force Manpower Standards
ARSR	Air Route Surveillance Radar
ARTCC	Air Route Traffic Control Center
ASR	Airport Surveillance Radar
ASTARS	AVS Staffing Tool and Reporting System
ATC	Air Traffic Control
ATCBI	Air Traffic Control Beacon Interrogators
ATSS	Airway Transportation Systems Specialists
AVS	Office of Aviation Safety
CMMS	Computerized Maintenance Management Software
DME	Distance Measuring Equipment
ESU	Environmental Support Unit
FAA	Federal Aviation Administration
FSEP	Facility, Service, and Equipment Profile
FTE	full-time equivalent
FY	fiscal year
GNAS	General National Airspace System
GNSS	Global Navigation Satellite System

HSI	human-systems integration
ILS	Instrument Landing System
LCOM	Logistics Composite Model
LDR	Labor Distribution Reporting
MIT	Miles-in-Trail
MON	Minimum Operational Network (of VORs)
NAS	National Airspace System
NAVAID	navigational aid
NextGen	Next Generation Air Transportation System
OCC	Operations Control Center
OJT	on-the-job training
OPM	Office of Personnel Management
PASS	Professional Aviation Safety Specialist
PFD	personal, fatigue, and delay (time)
PFF	Precommission Facility File
POD	process-oriented description
RMLS	Remote Monitoring and Logging System
RMM	Remote Maintenance Monitoring
SOC	Service Operations Center
SOC/OCC	Service Operations Center/Operations Control Center
SSC	System Support Center
TRACON	Terminal Radar Approach Control
VOR	VHF Omnidirectional Range
VOR/DME	VHF Omnidirectional Range/Distance Measuring Equipment
VV&A	verification, validation, and acceptance
WBS	work breakdown structure
WSSAS	Windows Staffing Standards Analysis System

Summary

Within the Federal Aviation Administration (FAA), the Airway Transportation Systems Specialists (ATSS) personnel maintain and certify the equipment in the National Airspace System (NAS). According to the definitions set forth by the Office of Management and Budget in Circular A-76, the certification work of ATSS is considered to be "inherently governmental"; that is, tasks performed to maintain and certify the NAS may only be performed by federal government (in this situation, FAA) employees. The Technical Operations service unit of the FAA includes more than 9,000 employees, two-thirds of whom are ATSS personnel.[1] In fiscal year 2012, Technical Operations had a budget of $1.7 billion. Thus, Technical Operations includes approximately 19 percent of the total FAA employees and less than 12 percent of the $15.9 billion total FAA budget (DOT, 2012).

Technical Operations comprises ATSS workers at five different types of Air Traffic Control (ATC) facilities: (1) Air Route Traffic Control Centers, also known as En Route Centers, track aircraft once they travel beyond the terminal airspace and reach cruising altitude; they include Service Operations Centers that coordinate work and monitor equipment. (2) Terminal Radar Approach Control (TRACON) facilities control air traffic as aircraft ascend from and descend to airports, generally covering a radius of about 40 miles around the primary airport; a TRACON facility also includes a Service Operations Center. (3) Core Airports, also called Operational Evolution Partnership airports, are the nation's busiest airports. (4) The General National Airspace System (GNAS) includes the facilities located outside the larger airport locations, including rural airports and equipment not based at any airport. (5) Operations Control Centers are the facilities that coordinate maintenance work and monitor equipment for a Service Area (Eastern, Central, Western) in the United States (Grant Thornton, 2011).[2]

[1]Rich McCormick, director, Labor Analysis, FAA, presentation to the Committee on Staffing Needs of Systems Specialists in Aviation, October 19, 2012.

[2]Ibid.

BOX S-1
Statement of Task

An ad hoc committee will conduct a study of the assumptions and methods used by the Federal Aviation Administration (FAA) to estimate staffing needs for FAA systems specialists to ensure proper maintenance and certification of the national airspace system. The committee will review available information on (A) the duties of employees in job series 2101 (Airways Transportation Systems Specialist) in the Technical Operations service unit; (B) the Professional Aviation Safety Specialists (PASS) union of the AFL-CIO; (C) the present-day staffing models employed by the FAA; (D) any materials already produced by the FAA including a recent gap analysis on staffing requirements; (E) current research on best staffing models for safety; and (F) non-U.S. staffing standards for employees in similar roles. Additionally, the FAA will assist in the committee's efforts by identifying relevant stakeholder organizations and agencies and facilitating communication with them. Based on its analysis of the available information, the committee will produce a report that will include

- a description and evaluation of current FAA staffing models and standards for systems specialists;
- recommendations for objective staffing standards that will maintain the safety of the National Airspace System going forward; and
- recommendations for the steps needed to transition from the current staffing models and approaches used by the FAA to the plans for staffing recommended by the committee.

At each facility, the ATSS personnel execute both tasks that are scheduled and predictable (e.g., performing regular preventive maintenance, conducting scheduled certification of equipment and facilities of the NAS, upgrading equipment, standing watch[3]) and tasks that are stochastic[4] and unpredictable in occurrence (e.g., detecting an adverse event or outage and then repairing and returning certified equipment to use after the event). These tasks are common across the five ATSS disciplines: (1) Communications, maintaining the systems that allow air traffic controllers and pilots to be in contact throughout the flight; (2) Surveillance and Radar, maintaining the systems that allow air traffic controllers to see the specific locations of all the aircraft in the airspace they are monitoring; (3) Automation, maintaining the systems that allow air traffic controllers to track each aircraft's current and future position, speed, and altitude; (4) Navigation, maintaining the systems that allow pilots to take off, maintain their course, approach, and land their aircraft; and (5) Environmental, maintaining the power, lighting, and heating/air conditioning systems at the ATC facilities (FAA, 2011b). Because the NAS needs to be available and reliable all the time, each of the different equipment systems includes redundancy so an outage can be fixed without disrupting the NAS.

The 2012 FAA Modernization and Reform Act mandated the National Research Council to appoint an ad hoc committee to study the assumptions and methods the FAA uses to estimate the number of ATSS personnel needed. This committee was appointed with the statement of task shown in Box S-1.

Rather than establish a standard for staffing models (a staffing model can be used to estimate the number of ATSS employees needed to fulfill the FAA's mission), the committee decided to identify relevant factors and considerations necessary to create a model that will yield a staffing number by a reasoned, scientifically sound approach. To accomplish its tasks, the committee received briefings and

[3]"Standing watch" refers to monitoring for adverse events and unscheduled outages of the equipment.

[4]Randomly determined; having a random probability distribution or pattern that may be analyzed statistically but may not be predicted.

materials from the FAA and the union representing ATSS personnel, Professional Aviation Safety Specialists (PASS). It also visited several ATC facilities, collected stakeholder input via a public webpage (most comments came from ATSS personnel), and examined several staffing models and the factors that are necessary input into the models. These models and the framework of human-systems integration (HSI) factors guided the committee's deliberations and its assessment of various modeling approaches. In the context of this report, a model depicts how different factors such as workload level or equipment repair time interact to determine optimal staffing levels (NRC, 2006).

STAFFING FACTORS AND MODEL CRITERIA

In addition to the inherent mix of scheduled and unpredictable tasks performed by ATSS personnel, staffing needs are further complicated by the FAA's planned implementation of the Next Generation Air Transportation System, or NextGen, which will continue to integrate new technology with current systems in the NAS. Input received from various stakeholders, along with the information received from the FAA regarding the primary factors to consider when developing a staffing model, informed the committee's work. One of the committee's major tasks was to identify the factors that should be included in the model; these related not only to manpower staffing but also to the human resources aspects that feed into modeling. The following nine factors were identified:

1. The time required for new hires, as well as ATSS personnel who are certifying on new equipment, to complete formal training at the FAA training center in Oklahoma City; the time required for them to receive on-the-job training (OJT) from more experienced ATSS personnel and complete the certification activities; and the increased workload on ATSS personnel who provide OJT
2. The distance an ATSS employee must travel to some remote facilities and the time required to make the trip
3. The potential environmental challenges involved in maintaining equipment that is near a hazardous area or located in places that experience severe weather
4. The time dedicated to serving in the military reserves or taking other forms of leave, including family and medical leave
5. The ability of ATSS personnel to meet all the job demands on their time without being unduly fatigued
6. Safety requirements that include the need to have two (or more) workers in some situations (e.g., working on high-voltage equipment)
7. Problems with the current FAA time reporting systems, such as Labor Distribution Reporting and the Remote Monitoring and Logging System, which provide data that are deficient for estimating the time ATSS personnel spend on daily tasks
8. Upcoming retirements from an aging workforce[5]
9. Other requirements on ATSS personnel time, such as nontechnical training and administrative tasks

In addition to identifying the factors to consider when building an accurate staffing model, the committee reviewed critical steps in the modeling process, including all of the following steps:

[5]The committee notes that attrition/accession models are best handled as separate human resources algorithms based upon the staffing model targets.

1. Following a comprehensive study and design process that incorporates the major workload factors at an appropriate level of detail, links workload to the time required to complete the tasks, and completes the six steps of the logical design process (i.e., feasibility, familiarization, measurement design, measurement, analysis and model selection, and implementation)
2. Incorporating key model considerations, including choosing the right type of model to use all relevant input and provide all required outputs
3. Attending to quality factors, such as ensuring that the model is transparent, scalable, easy to use, relevant, and valid (NRC, 2006:33)

The committee used the above criteria to examine existing ATSS staffing models including the Windows Staffing Standards Analysis System (WSSAS) and the Tech Ops District Model. Although these models meet some of the criteria, overall the committee found them lacking in some areas and recommends development of a new model using the steps and factors outlined in the report. The committee also reviewed recent efforts by FAA to examine its past modeling efforts and to assess its needs for future modeling through a contract with the Grant Thornton consulting firm. The Grant Thornton reports build on the WSSAS, which is a deterministic[6] model, and suggest improvements to the key data sources. Finally, the committee reviewed the steps necessary to successfully implement a new model, including estimates of the time needed for each activity (e.g., development, testing, preparation, implementation, validation, and monitoring results), as well as the role of FAA staff, funding requirements, and consideration of other resources within the model.

REPORT FINDINGS, CONCLUSIONS, AND RECOMMENDATIONS

The following findings, conclusions, and recommendations are shown in order of appearance in the report chapters and do not necessarily reflect their order of importance.

ATSS Staffing and NextGen

The Committee understands that the FAA's planned transition to NextGen is under way, but that the maintenance requirements are not yet publicly specified. An effective staffing model goes beyond documenting today's required ATSS staffing levels; instead, a robust and accessible staffing model should be capable of incorporating such additional inputs as they become available, not only with respect to NextGen but also with respect to inevitable continuing technological advances.

Finding 2-1: Changes to the NAS such as NextGen and Minimum Operational Network (MON) implementation and unspecified decommissioning policies all make the amount of work to be performed by ATSS personnel ambiguous and complicate the FAA's task in developing an appropriate staffing model for ATSS.

Conclusion 2-1: Developing and using a successful staffing model to predict future outcomes will be limited by unknowns such as decommissioning policies for legacy equipment, installation of NextGen equipment, and consolidation of facilities.

[6]A deterministic model is a mathematical function of multiple inputs such as the type of equipment and the nature of the task to be performed. That is, a single value of a model outcome variable can be derived from a set of values for all the input variables.

Recommendation 2-1: The FAA should ensure that ATSS staffing models will incorporate new information about the unknown factors that affect ATSS staffing such as NextGen as it becomes available, consider their staffing implications, and use appropriate modeling techniques to plan for contingencies.

Critical Factors Affecting ATSS Staffing

The job duties and work environment for ATSS personnel, represented by PASS, present special challenges and issues that should be addressed by an effective staffing model. By reviewing documents related to the job of the ATSS personnel and considering the perspectives of a wide array of stakeholders, including the systems specialists themselves, the committee identified several critical factors affecting demand for systems specialists that result not only from the unusual requirements of this particular job series but also from the demands placed on ATSS personnel by the external aviation environment. Although the committee focused much of its effort on the manpower domain, it noted several human resource areas to address.

Finding 2-2: A number of human resource issues, such as hiring procedures, training requirements, retirements, and military obligations, affect the number of qualified ATSS personnel who are available at any point in time to maintain the NAS.

Conclusion 2-2: The committee concludes that human resource issues such as retirements and succession planning considerations should be addressed in conjunction with any comprehensive manpower staffing model.

Recommendation 2-2: In accordance with the principles of human-systems integration, the FAA should build a robust staffing model that takes into account all of the following aspects of the ATSS job series, in addition to the time that ATSS personnel spend on preventive and corrective maintenance tasks:

- Training issues, time to schedule training, the time required to attend training, and the time of experienced ATSS personnel necessary to provide OJT
- Travel time to and from work sites
- Environmental challenges
- Time dedicated to military reserve service or family and medical leave
- Fatigue mitigation plans
- Safety factors
- Labor Distribution Reporting deficiencies and other data deficiencies
- Aging workforce and succession planning considerations
- FAA's Next Generation (NextGen) system
- Nontechnical task demands

The Staffing Modeling Process for ATSS

The committee had several discussions on what would be a valid and useful model and how it could estimate the number of ATSS personnel necessary for maintaining the NAS in a safe, efficient, and effective manner. These discussions did not focus on a total number of ATSS personnel, but there was an understanding that, should the model generate a number greater than 6,100, the anticipated FAA budget would need to be quickly increased to avoid negative implications for the safety and efficiency of the NAS. In that case the FAA would have to employ risk mitigation to compensate for the less than sufficient staffing while the requisite budget was approved and additional staff was hired, trained, and assigned to the appropriate sites.

Conclusion 3-1: Dedicated budget requirements for the ATSS personnel are likely to result from application of any comprehensive manpower staffing model and will need to be addressed.

Leaders of the model design and development process should intentionally look backward and forward during the phases of a logical design process so that the end result is logical, valid, and compliant with the stated purpose. In particular, data examination during the measurement and analysis phases may necessitate revised data collection procedures or additional research into some of the factors that affect ATSS staffing levels. Moreover, those who develop the model need to plan for future improvements to the model as modeling methodology and data collection procedures evolve and as the FAA obtains greater understanding of the causes of variability in the tasks performed by ATSS personnel. Insights gained at any phase can redirect the study in unexpected ways; thus, the study team needs to be not only flexible but also seasoned in handling unexpected situations and understanding which approaches are most likely to be effective in a given situation.

Recommendation 3-1: The FAA should execute a modeling process that allows for future improvements in data modeling techniques and applicability.

Assessment of the FAA's Previous Modeling Efforts for ATSS

To provide a sound basis for recommendations for future ATSS staffing models, the committee compared prior FAA staffing models and the Grant Thornton proposed modeling approach with each other and against the set of criteria for valid staffing models compiled by the committee. The deterministic WSSAS model was based on valid structure and suitable types of data and data sources. Essentially, the WSSAS incorporated the pieces of equipment at each site, the number of technician hours required for each corrective or preventive maintenance action on each piece of equipment, and the probability of failure for each type of equipment. These measures were combined to establish the maintenance workload for each piece of equipment, and workloads were summed across all equipment at a work site. Allowances were added for technician unavailability, and a factor was added for other required activities. Time data came from time studies and consensus judgments by subject matter experts, supplemented by contractor-provided times for new equipment. Neither the reliability of input data to the model nor the validity of the output staffing levels was measured. The reports generated were useful to supervisors and administrators, and the WSSAS model was reasonably transparent to all users. However, updating the model was expensive, and the lack of resources for updating eventually made the model unsustainable.

Conclusion 4-1: The approach represented by the original WSSAS model included many of the important variables (e.g., equipment counts and task durations together with failure rates and allowances) to determine the staffing required at each site.

Finding 4-1: The WSSAS model does not appear to contain stochastic elements in places where these may have been appropriate.

Finding 4-2: The WSSAS model made no prediction of outcomes such as the impact of staffing levels on NAS availability and safety.

The Tech Ops District Model is an allocation model only (that is, it aimed only at distributing available personnel resources effectively irrespective of their collective adequacy to maintain a safe and effective NAS), rather than a sufficiency model (i.e., a model designed to predict the resources needed to sustain system performances at an acceptable level). The committee therefore found it to not be an appropriate basis for moving forward toward a valid model for staffing. It is a regression model that only shows, at best, how a number of variables are related in a statistical manner to then-current staffing levels by district. The Tech Ops District Model was never validated against outcome measures. Any work regression model, without measurement of actual hours required to perform the task, will necessarily preserve the status quo in terms of staffing, so that the performance consequences will remain the same and may not meet current or future performance requirements. The committee recommended against using the Tech Ops District Model as a source of either the modeling framework or data for future work and did not consider it further as a basis for FAA staffing models.

Finding 4-3: The Tech Ops District Model was an allocation model and not a sufficiency staffing model.

Conclusion 4-2: The Tech Ops District Model is not an adequate framework for future work.

The Grant Thornton approach builds on the WSSAS model but suggests improvements to the key data sources for the future model. It appears to capture the relationships between equipment and maintenance staffing, and it has provisions for idiosyncratic factors (variances) affecting staffing. Although the Grant Thornton design represents distinct improvements over WSSAS, the committee has two concerns with an approach built on the basis of the WSSAS model. First, corrective maintenance in the ATSS job often occurs in an unscheduled, stochastic manner, and the WSSAS model does not account for the intrinsically stochastic nature of these events. Even if some elements like mean time between component failures can be predicted, some randomness or unpredictability remains, related to the timing and location of a specific failure requiring corrective maintenance. Before dismissing various probabilistic aspects of maintenance work and methods, these stochastic elements and their relationship to adequate and safe staffing levels need to be understood and thoroughly explored to determine if and how they should be included in the model design.

Second, like the WSSAS and Tech Ops District models, the proposed model does not predict the consequences or results of staffing at alternative levels. It would be advisable to gather data necessary to study stochastic properties of outages, required time to repair, and shift profile dynamics. It would also be helpful to explore potential linkages of key internal Technical Operations performance metrics to various levels of staffing allocations.

Finding 4-4: The Grant Thornton prospective model builds on the earlier WSSAS model, and thus inherits some of its strengths and limitations. Its strengths include the same elemental data structure, supplemented with more recent data partly derived from existing data bases.

Conclusion 4-3: Based on the latest description of the proposed model in the Grant Thornton report, the limitation of the Grant Thornton approach is the plan for a deterministic model that does not consider the implications of stochastic elements. Further, it makes no predictions of outcome measures such as NAS equipment availability and safety.

Future Modeling for ATSS Staffing

The committee applied the modeling approaches and criteria developed in this report from staffing model knowledge to the WSSAS model, the Tech Ops District Model, and the proposed Grant Thornton approach to modeling. First, the factual basis of the three models was tabulated and assessed in terms of the criteria. Next, other sources of successful modeling in similar situations were assessed for the insights they might add to the future models of ATSS staffing developed by the FAA.

The committee can summarize the attributes and the evaluation of models based on these attributes as a set of statements about what are good criteria for the FAA's future modeling efforts. The best science currently available supports the following recommendations for a valid and usable model.

Recommendation 4-1: The FAA should develop a new ATSS staffing model based on the modeling framework and criteria developed in this report. The model should be developed using a model structure that is based on equipment inventory, failure rates, and time to perform each task and should include any valid allowances and accommodations. The model structure should include both deterministic and stochastic estimates for variables such as task duration, as appropriate. The developed model structure should be based on the different specialties of ATSS technicians, rather than providing just an overall staffing level at each facility.

Recommendation 4-2: The FAA should develop a model that captures stochastic elements, unless it can be demonstrated that stochastic aspects of the maintenance process have no material effect on the staffing. For example, some tasks may exhibit multiple deterministic durations of identifiable elements, rather than strictly stochastic durations.

Recommendation 4-3: The FAA should incorporate data for the model that are appropriate to the duration and frequency of the tasks modeled and to its data collection capabilities. Specifically, the FAA needs a process to systematically validate through direct observation both historical estimates of task durations and estimates by subject matter experts.

Recommendation 4-4: The FAA should ensure that the ongoing data collection and input essential for model use do not place an unacceptable burden on data providers.

Recommendation 4-5: The FAA should ensure that output reports from the system predict consequences such as overall NAS availability time, deferred preventive maintenance activities, and overtime required.

Recommendation 4-6: The FAA should ensure that output reports are tailored closely to the needs of FAA's internal users at multiple organizational levels, in order to increase transparency of, and user trust in, the model.

Implementing a Future Model for ATSS Staffing

The committee discusses six steps, each of which comprises a number of activities that should be undertaken to increase the likelihood of a successful model launch. Each activity requires time and resources. Ideally, the FAA and its staffing model experts would add to these major steps as needed and elaborate on each, specifying what needs to be done by whom and creating a schedule to be followed for each step.

Step 1 includes all the activities associated with the actual development of the model. Step 2 involves a pretest of the model prior to full implementation, comparing it to five criteria by which a staffing model should be evaluated: transparency, scalability, usability, relevance, and validity. As review and improvement of the staffing model is a continuous process, these five criteria should be kept in mind once the model is implemented and is being validated and amended.

Step 3 focuses on the activities necessary to prepare the FAA to transition from the current state of staffing to a new process for establishing staffing levels via a carefully constructed staffing model. The FAA will need to develop a detailed plan to *implement* the new staffing model and create the timeline for the transition, checking to see what other events might affect the implementation. Step 4 encompasses the actual implementation and rollout of the model according to the plans laid out in Step 3, all of which should logically be synchronized with key FAA human resources, training, and budget processes to the extent possible. Step 5 is the post-implementation evaluation of the quality of the staffing model against the five standards of transparency, scalability, usability, relevance, and validity. All of the quality standards are important, but validity is perhaps the most critical. Unless the results of the staffing plan allow the FAA to maintain the NAS, nothing else is relevant.

Recommendation 5-1: The FAA should prepare a timeline that details all the activities associated with model development and implementation that must be completed and should ensure that the resources necessary to accomplish each are available.

Step 6 includes the activities that are necessary to sustain the model over a period of time: monitor the staffing model, evaluate its adequacy, and make adjustments as needed. The staffing model that is produced as a result of this study will be more effective if it is periodically reviewed and updated to reflect the changing environment of ATSS work. If a review indicates that the staffing model is outdated, modifications should be made and the cycle of implementation should begin anew. An effective and useful modeling process takes into account the lessons that have accrued from each round of the implementation process and incorporates them into the next iteration of the staffing model, resulting in a spiral development process.

Recommendation 5-2: Once implemented, the FAA should continue to monitor the effectiveness of the staffing model by collecting data from multiple sources and should make adjustments as needed to enhance the accuracy of the model. In addition, the model should be adapted as changes to the major components of the model are made, such as changes in the tasks performed, equipment used, and training processes.

1

Background and Overview

INTRODUCTION

The National Airspace System (NAS) is the integrated network of components necessary to manage the United States airspace effectively and safely: air navigation facilities, equipment, services, airports or landing areas, aeronautical charts, information technology, rules, regulations, procedures, technical information, manpower, and material. The Federal Aviation Administration (FAA) owns and operates the air traffic control systems in the NAS. Some of these system components (e.g., navigational aids and radar facilities) are also used by the U.S. Department of Defense and Department of Homeland Security in their missions. The NAS continues to evolve as the characteristics of aircraft (e.g., speed and altitude capabilities); their communication and navigation equipment; and the ground equipment used for communication, tracking, and guidance evolve and as the usage of the airspace continues to increase, including the future addition of drone traffic.

The maintenance of the NAS is the responsibility of the Airway Transportation Systems Specialists (ATSS) (job series 2101) who work for the Technical Operations branch of the FAA Air Traffic Organization. The organization chart in Figure 1-1, from FAA Notice 1100.332, presents the management hierarchy for Technical Operations within the Air Traffic Organization and its lines of reporting (FAA, 2012a).

Throughout the history of the FAA, the certification and oversight of the NAS has been considered to be *inherently governmental* (FAA, 2011a; Office of Management and Budget, 2003). Almost 50 years ago, the Office of Management and Budget published Circular A-76, *Performance of Commercial Activities*, which defines "inherently governmental activity" as "any activity that is so intimately related to the public interest as to mandate performance by government personnel" (Office of Management and Budget, 2003).

On December 7, 2000, President Clinton issued Executive Order 13180, Air Traffic Performance Based Organization, to establish a more businesslike, customer service focused FAA. Executive Order 13180 specifically states that air traffic services are inherently governmental (U.S. Government Printing Office, 2000). However, on June 4, 2002, President Bush issued Executive Order 13264, which amended

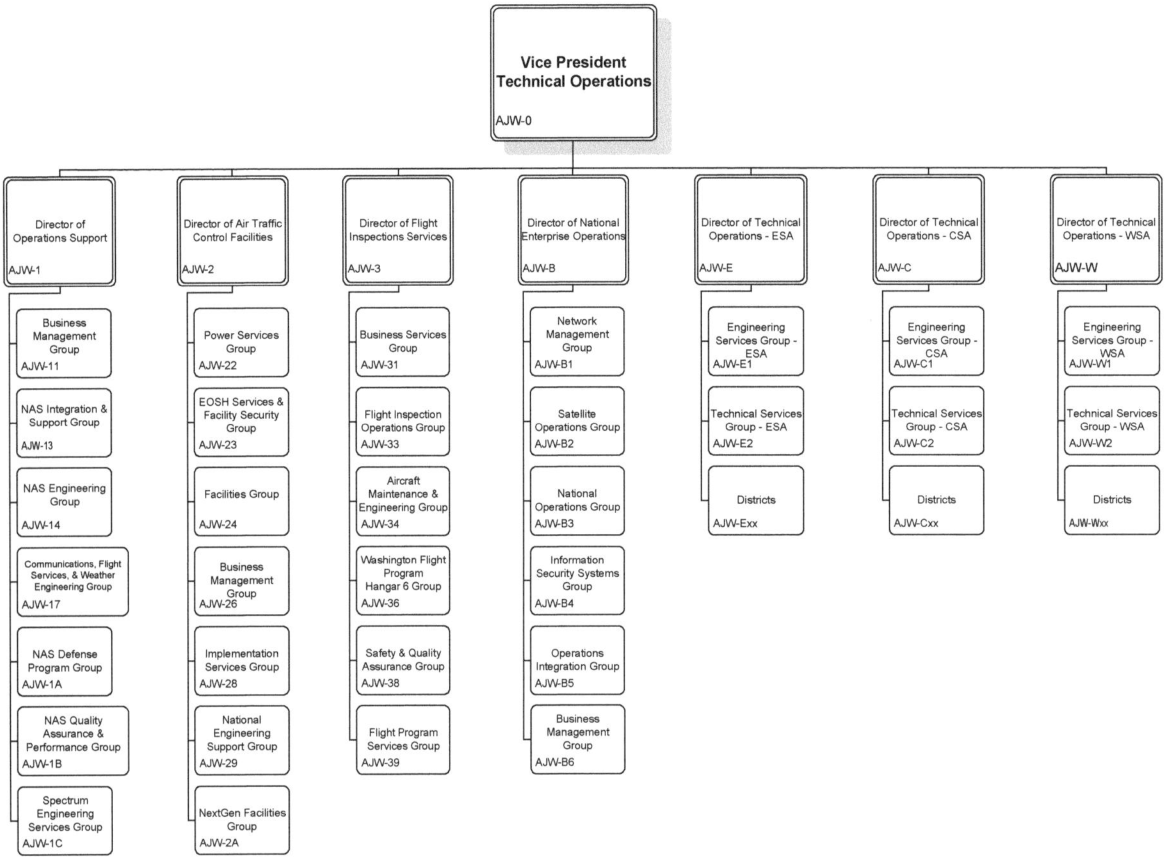

FIGURE 1-1 FAA air traffic organization, Technical Operations organizational chart.
SOURCE: FAA, 2012a:25.

Executive Order 13180 and deleted the term "inherently governmental function" from the original order (U.S. Government Printing Office, 2002). This amendment allowed the FAA to contract some air traffic controller functions to private concerns, largely at smaller air traffic control towers (Wigfall, 2006). Maintenance and certification of NAS equipment, however, remained a strictly governmental function that is performed only by the FAA. Consequently, this study focuses only on employees of the FAA.

Airway Transportation Systems Specialists

President Obama's 2013 FAA budget submission describes the responsibilities of the FAA Technical Operations branch, and specifically of ATSS, as follows:

> Technical Operations ensures that thousands of systems, facilities, and pieces of equipment are operationally ready to manage our nation's air traffic control system. Without system specialists and management teams working to complete preventive maintenance and repair down equipment, unscheduled outages can result in delays in the system, negatively impacting the flying public.
>
> Another component of the Technical Operations organization that serves as a vital link in delivering air traffic control services is Aviation System Standards' flight inspection operations. Technical Operations

employees conduct airborne inspection of electronic signals from ground-based NAVAIDs [navigational aids] to support aircraft departure, en route, and arrival procedures. This group evaluates flight procedures for accuracy, human factors fly-ability, and obstacle clearance. Without this "check," the NAS would not be as safe as it is today.

Technical Operations manages their operations by measuring performance of the NAS based on what Systems or services are available for air traffic control operations (Adjusted Operational Availability). However, this metric directly impacts FAA's airport capability metric (Average Daily Airport capacity) as noted above, as well as our safety reduction goals (Commercial and General Aviation Fatal Accident Rates). Technical Operations ensures that terminal and en route controllers have all critical parts of the NAS infrastructure available for the safety and efficient delivery of air traffic services. (Department of Transportation, 2012:23)

The Technical Operations service unit of the FAA includes more than 9,000 employees, two-thirds of whom are ATSS personnel.[1] In fiscal year 2012, Technical Operations had a budget of $1.7 billion. Thus, Technical Operations includes approximately 19 percent of the total FAA employees and less than 12 percent of the $15.9 billion total FAA budget (DOT, 2012).

There are five types types of facilities in Technical Operations: (1) Air Route Traffic Control Centers, also known as En Route centers, which track aircraft once they travel beyond the terminal airspace and reach cruising altitude and include Service Operations Centers that coordinate work and monitor equipment; (2) Terminal Radar Approach Control (TRACON) facilities, which control air traffic as aircraft ascend from and descend to airports and generally cover a radius of about 40 miles around the primary airport, which also include a Service Operations Center; (3) Core Airports (or Operational Evolution Partnership airports), the nation's busiest airports; (4) the General National Airspace System, comprising the facilities located outside the larger locations, including rural airports and equipment not based at any airport; and (5) Operations Control Centers, the facilities that coordinate work and monitor equipment for a Service Area (Eastern, Central, Western) in the United States (Grant Thornton, 2011).[2]

One general position description covers all ATSS employees in Job Series 2101 in the Technical Operations unit of FAA's Air Traffic Organization:

Airway Transportation Systems Specialists (ATSS) install and maintain electronic equipment and lighting aids associated with facilities and services required for aviation navigation to ensure a reliable, safe, and smooth flow of air traffic. This involves work with radar, communications, computers, navigational aids, airport lighting aids, and electrical/mechanical support for facilities on and off airports within the network of the National Airspace System. It includes periodic maintenance (inspection and analysis of equipment with associated adjustments), corrective maintenance, troubleshooting, repair and replacement of malfunctioning equipment, and certification. ATSS may be required to maintain entire facilities, including electronic equipment, electrical power distribution, emergency backup power, power conditioning systems, and heating, ventilation and air conditioning systems. Many ATSS work out of offices located at or near airports and on service equipment located on airports, in air traffic control towers, automated flight service stations, air route traffic control centers, in open fields, or even on remote mountain tops.[3]

ATSS personnel maintain equipment and services of the NAS in the three Service Areas (Eastern, Central, and Western) throughout the United States, Guam, American Samoa, and Puerto Rico. All ATSS positions are covered by a collective bargaining agreement with the Professional Aviation Safety Special-

---

[1]Rich McCormick, director, Labor Analysis, FAA, presentation on Labor Analysis to the Committee on Staffing Needs of Systems Specialists in Aviation, October 19, 2012.

[2]Ibid.

[3]ATSS posting found at https://www.usajobs.gov/GetJob/ViewDetails/313337100 [May 2013].

ists (PASS), a labor union of the American Federation of Labor-Congress of Industrial Organizations. The most recent collective bargaining agreement was ratified on December 16, 2012.

Roles and Duties

ATSS personnel are employed at a variety of facilities throughout the United States and its territories, ranging from small airports to large TRACON facilities and major airports. All facilities need all specialties to cover the equipment, although smaller facilities may use more multi-certified ATSS personnel while larger facilities will have many ATSS personnel with deeper skills in individual specialties. The ATSS work is composed primarily of four types of tasks:

1. Performing scheduled (daily, weekly, monthly, etc.) preventive maintenance on equipment
2. Standing watch for detection of adverse events and unscheduled outages (while working on other tasks)
3. Returning equipment to service following an unplanned outage and after certification
4. Performing upgrades and equipment changes as the NAS evolves

This work is carried out inside the tower/TRACON, at a closely adjacent airfield, or at a remote location. At smaller facilities, the ATSS personnel typically schedule their own daily tasks based on the list of required scheduled maintenance or any equipment that is out of service and needs to be repaired immediately. Priority of tasks depends on the safety of the traveling public and is typically set by understanding the impact of equipment outages on the NAS and the deadlines for preventive maintenance or upgrading equipment. ATSS personnel interact with each other to provide support across specialties, communicating directly rather than through a hierarchy. Facilities of different sizes use different management structures. At facilities with larger staffs, there is more direct coordination by management, while at smaller facilities work is more likely to be coordinated by the ATSS personnel themselves. At any facility, the ATSS personnel performing a task can call on technical back-up at two levels—either experienced technicians with a great deal of knowledge or engineers with even more detailed knowledge—although these personnel may not be immediately available at all hours.[4]

ATSS personnel may pursue certification in five technical disciplines: Communication, Environmental, Navaid, Surveillance, and Automation (FAA, 2011b). Most ATSS will continue with additional training over their careers in Technical Operations in order to diversify their skills and certify in multiple disciplines.

ORIGIN OF STUDY AND STATEMENT OF TASK

In February 2012, the FAA Modernization and Reform Act of 2012 (H.R. 658) was signed by President Barack Obama.[5] This law contained requests for studies to be conducted by the National Academy of Sciences, including a study of the methods and accompanying assumptions of the FAA used to estimate its staffing needs for FAA systems specialists, referred to in this document as "ATSS." In the operational context, ATSS personnel are also referred to as "systems specialists" and as "2101s," the latter being a reference to their Office of Personnel Management job classification. In response to one of these requests, the National Research Council of the National Academies appointed an ad hoc committee in September

[4]Comments submitted to Staffing Needs of Systems Specialists in Aviation Stakeholder webpage, 2013.

[5]H.R. 658, 112th Congress: FAA Modernization and Reform Act of 2012. Available: http://www.govtrack.us/congress/bills/112/hr658 [June 2013].

BOX 1-1
Statement of Task

An ad hoc committee will conduct a study of the assumptions and methods used by the Federal Aviation Administration (FAA) to estimate staffing needs for FAA systems specialists to ensure proper maintenance and certification of the national airspace system. The committee will review available information on (A) the duties of employees in job series 2101 (Airways Transportation Systems Specialist) in the Technical Operations service unit; (B) the Professional Aviation Safety Specialists (PASS) union of the AFL-CIO; (C) the present-day staffing models employed by the FAA; (D) any materials already produced by the FAA including a recent gap analysis on staffing requirements; (E) current research on best staffing models for safety; and (F) non-U.S. staffing standards for employees in similar roles. Additionally, the FAA will assist in the committee's efforts by identifying relevant stakeholder organizations and agencies and facilitating communication with them. Based on its analysis of the available information, the committee will produce a report that will include

- a description and evaluation of current FAA staffing models and standards for systems specialists;
- recommendations for objective staffing standards that will maintain the safety of the National Airspace System going forward; and
- recommendations for the steps needed to transition from the current staffing models and approaches used by the FAA to the plans for staffing recommended by the committee.

2012 composed of members representing multiple disciplines. The task of this Committee on Staffing Needs of Systems Specialists in Aviation (hereafter, "the committee") is presented in Box 1-1.

At the first meeting of the committee on October 18-19, 2012, the FAA gave additional guidance regarding the task at hand, informing the committee that a contract between PASS, the labor union that represents ATSS employees, and the FAA would be ratified and that the staffing level of 6,100, although arbitrary, would remain in place for the first 16 months of the new contract.[6] The FAA representatives also noted that this number was a base for staffing levels and not a ceiling. The FAA explained in a later meeting that the agreement called for a "scientifically valid" model to be used to determine the optimal staffing level for the ATSS class of workers. In discussions with representatives of the FAA, the committee clarified another requirement of the task, the request for recommendations for objective staffing standards that will maintain the safety of the NAS going forward. Rather than establish a standard for staffing models (i.e., the number of ATSS employees needed to fulfill the FAA's mission), the committee was asked to identify relevant factors and considerations necessary to create a model that will yield a staffing number.

SCOPE AND COMMITTEE APPROACH

The scope of the committee's task was to review relevant FAA reports, data models, performance metrics, surveys, job descriptions, and information about staffing models from other sources and to engage the FAA, PASS, ATSS personnel, and other stakeholders of the FAA to achieve the stated goals. Stakeholders (see Table 1-1) were identified by the FAA,[7] and input was requested from several primary

[6]The contract vote by PASS had been held and approved prior to the first committee meeting.

[7]Stakeholder list prepared by FAA staff and sent by Rich McCormick, director, Labor Analysis, FAA, to the committee on November 28, 2012.

TABLE 1-1 Stakeholders Identified by the FAA

Stakeholder	Category
Air Traffic Management	Primary
Professional Aviation Safety Specialists (PASS)	Primary
National Air Traffic Controllers Association (NATCA)	Primary
National Association of Government Employees (NAGE)	Primary
Flight Standards	Primary
Flight Inspections	Primary
Federal Aviation Administration (FAA) Academy	Primary
General Aviation	Secondary
U.S. Congress	Secondary
Flight Services Stations	Secondary
Airlines	Secondary
Airports	Secondary
Airport Authorities	Secondary
Regional Administrators	Secondary
Nonfederal Towers	Secondary
Other Federal Departments	Secondary
Department of the Interior—Fisheries and Wildlife Services	
Department of Commerce—National Weather Service	
Department of Defense—National Defense Program Office	
General Aviation	
Foreign Governments	Secondary

stakeholders, primarily those who could be contacted directly. In addition, a webpage was set up for public comment. Most of the respondents were ATSS personnel. The committee also conducted site visits to observe the work of ATSS personnel in context, to better understand the requirements of the job.

As noted, the committee identified a number of sources of information relevant to achieving its goals, including documents, discussions, research literature, and committee members' observations at selected facilities. The documents reviewed included job descriptions of 2101s in the Technical Operations service unit, FAA documentation providing targets and performance outcomes, and information collected from the union that represents the ATSS personnel, PASS. Information on staffing models and standards used in other countries was also requested but not received. Additionally, information was gathered at committee meetings in the form of presentations and discussions by FAA headquarters staff, contractors, and PASS representatives who shared and discussed current staffing concerns and other challenges. The committee reviewed staffing models for similar jobs and studied the manner in which these models integrated safety and efficiency parameters, as well as the approaches used to develop such models. As detailed below, several facilities were visited to discuss relevant issues with ATSS and related personnel, including site visits at Leesburg, Dulles, Los Angeles International, Greenville-Spartanburg, and Buffalo.

During the first meeting on October 18-19, 2012, in Washington, DC, the FAA discussed the need for the study and the key factors that the FAA's representatives felt needed to be addressed in a staffing model. The committee deliberated on next steps in the formulation of future meeting agendas and site visits to better understand the key activities to be conducted for this study.

The second meeting of the committee was held on December 6-7, 2012, in Washington, DC. The committee visited two sites on December 7, 2012, to further explore workload factors through discussion with Technical Operations personnel and to develop a contextual understanding of the tasks conducted by ATSS employees in the course of daily operations. The two sites were the Washington Center in

Leesburg, Virginia, and Washington Dulles International Airport Tower in Dulles, Virginia. The third meeting was held on January 23-24, 2013, in Washington, DC, and focused on report writing and content updates. An FAA question and answer session was held at this meeting to gain additional information and clarifications and to answer questions that were still pending from previous sessions. At the fourth meeting, held on February 27-28, 2013, in Irvine, California, the committee focused on writing its report. In addition to the committee meetings, individual members completed site visits at the following FAA locations: Buffalo, New York; Greenville, South Carolina; and Los Angeles, California.

IMPORTANCE OF HUMAN-SYSTEMS INTEGRATION

The committee discussed several guiding principles to help identify the parameters and models to define the ATSS workload and establish appropriate staffing levels. These included human-resources manpower and personnel models, management systems models using operations research and optimization formulas, and the FAA's traditional models, which were currently in use. The committee agreed that an understanding of the relationships among the system components and the workforce was critical to an integrative effort toward optimizing staffing relative to workload. The committee conceptualized the maintenance of the NAS as a complex, dynamic system with significant interdependencies among all system components, including the ATSS personnel who maintain them. The committee drew mainly from the human-systems integration (HSI) framework because of its history and use across aviation, defense, aerospace, medical, and other complex organizational systems for the past three decades.

The HSI framework requires that no one component of a system should be considered in isolation; the careful integration of all systems components maximizes outcomes related to the pursuit of increased safety and heightened performance (Booher, 2003; National Research Council, 2007). In a traditional HSI framework, the system comprises multiple domains such as manpower, personnel, training, survivability, safety, occupational health, environment, habitability, and human factors engineering (U.S. Air Force, undated). To fulfill the charge of the committee and make recommendations regarding the FAA Systems Specialists, the focus in this report is on exploring the domains of manpower, personnel, safety, and training. With respect to addressing workforce needs, the committee felt that the interdependence of these four areas was particularly relevant to the statement of task. The consideration of environmental factors in Chapter 2 is a direct consequence of using an HSI framework. It is the committee's judgment that the absence of a viable manpower model has undermined the FAA's capability to systematically apply an HSI-centered approach across all domains. A conceptual model of HSI is illustrated in Figure 1-2 (U.S. Air Force, undated).

STRUCTURE OF THIS REPORT

This report contains five chapters. This chapter provided an overview of the ATSS job and the context in which it is performed; it also introduces the HSI framework, which guided the committee's considerations. Chapter 2 discusses inputs received from stakeholders related to the variables that should be included in a staffing model for the ATSS job. It also contains a more detailed synopsis of the committee's understanding of the role of ATSS personnel. Chapter 3 presents criteria and characteristics of good staffing models in general and in particular as they apply to ATSS personnel. In Chapter 4, the committee evaluates past FAA staffing models according to the criteria discussed. Chapter 5 concludes with a discussion of the steps the FAA needs to transition to a future model that conforms to the committee's recommendations.

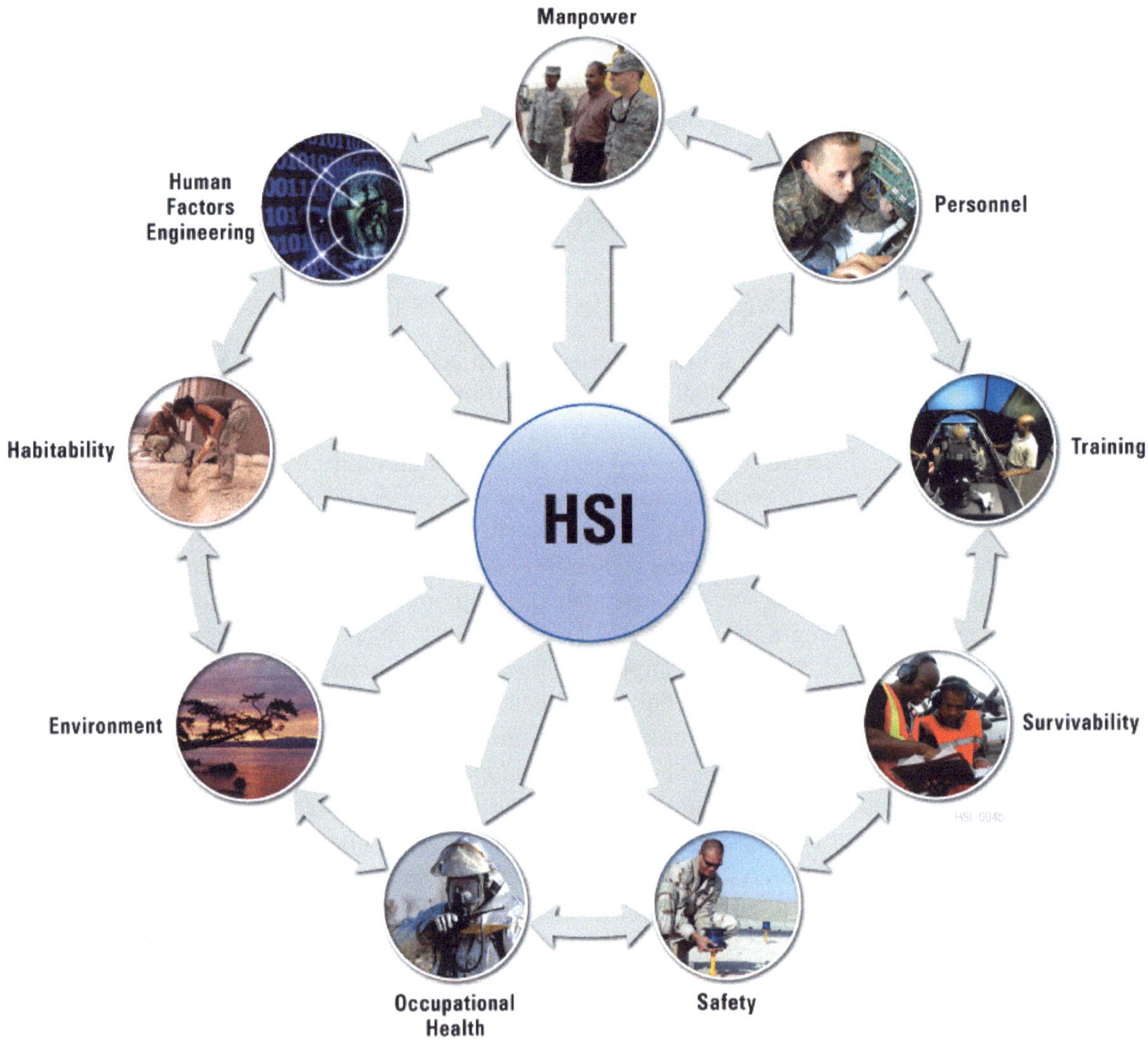

FIGURE 1-2 A conceptual model of human-systems integration.
SOURCE: U.S. Air Force, undated.

2

Work Environment Considerations for Airway Transportation Systems Specialists

The job duties and work environment for Airway Transportation Systems Specialists (ATSS) present special challenges and issues that should be addressed by an effective staffing model for ATSS. By reviewing documents related to the job of the ATSS personnel and considering the perspectives of a wide array of stakeholders, including the systems specialists themselves, the committee identified several critical factors affecting demand for systems specialists that result not only from the unusual requirements of this particular job series but also from the demands placed on incumbents in the job by the external aviation environment.

This chapter first reviews factors related to the current design of the ATSS job that will have a direct bearing on staffing. It then reviews the information obtained from systems specialists and various stakeholder groups, from presentations and documents, and from a public webpage for collecting comments related to the tasks ATSS personnel perform and to other demands on their time. The criteria for effective performance as well as the consequences of failure are discussed. The chapter also contains an overview of other major factors that should be considered as the Federal Aviation Administration (FAA) develops models to guide the systems specialist staffing process.

OVERVIEW

ATSS personnel are assigned to the Technical Operations branch of the FAA's Air Traffic Organization and are deployed across the United States as they maintain elements of the National Airspace System (NAS). ATSS employees can be collocated where concentrations of facilities and equipment reside or in teams that travel to support NAS components widely scattered throughout their geographic areas of responsibility. The NAS itself is divided into three major geographic service areas for the purpose of equipment maintenance: Eastern, Central, and Western. As Figure 2-1 shows, within each of these three areas, ATSS personnel are assigned to System Support Centers (SSCs) and support five types of work sites within Technical Operations: Air Route Traffic Control Centers (ARTCCs), Terminal Radar

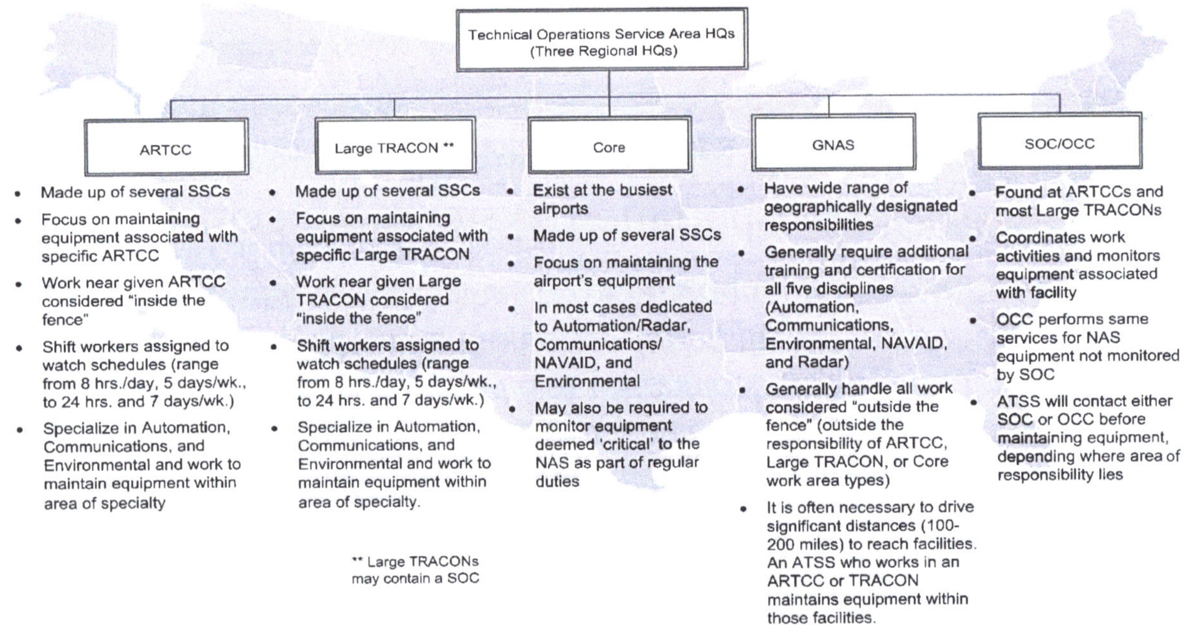

FIGURE 2-1 Overview of the Technical Operations organization.
SOURCE: Rich McCormick, director, Labor Analysis, FAA, ATSS Briefing for the National Academy of Sciences. Presentation to the Committee on Staffing Needs of Systems Specialists in Aviation, October 19, 2012. All disciplines, including NAVAIDs (navigational aids), are explained in the section on Discipline Types and Staff Substitution.

Approach Control (TRACON) facilities, Core Airports,[1] the General National Airspace System (GNAS), and Service Operation Centers/Operations Control Centers (SOCs/OCCs).[2]

ATSS personnel certify equipment and services to ensure the safety and performance of the NAS. To accomplish this responsibility, ATSS personnel perform two major functions: (1) scheduled preventive maintenance activities, including inspections to ensure continued certification of equipment as well as the installation and certification of new equipment; and (2) unscheduled, corrective maintenance and subsequent certification of repaired equipment, often on an emergency basis when equipment fails (FAA, 2011a). A third, ancillary function is the supervision of both installation of new equipment and decommissioning of old equipment. The GNAS work site typically has the lead for these activities, but the SSCs at the TRACON facilities and ARTCCs support these activities as well. There are other required tasks and activities—for example, training, administrative duties, and recordkeeping.

[1]The FAA uses the term "Core" for a list of approximately 30 high-activity airports. For example, "the 30 CORE airports presently handle 63 percent of the country's passengers and 68 percent of its operations" according to discussions recorded in *Federal Register* 77(119) (Wednesday, June 20, 2012). Available: http://www.gpo.gov/fdsys/pkg/FR-2012-06-20/html/2012-14893.htm [June 2013].

[2]Rich McCormick, director, Labor Analysis, FAA. ATSS Briefing for the National Academy of Sciences. Presentation to the Committee on Staffing Needs of Systems Specialists in Aviation, October 19, 2012

Based on observations of task performance, it is clear that ATSS personnel rely on highly developed skills for many tasks. In addition, ATSS personnel rely on reasoning at the rule-based level (e.g., following a written procedure for preventive maintenance on radar) and the knowledge-based level (e.g., understanding why an out-of-specification reading is occurring) (Rasmussen, 1983). The former requires valid procedure descriptions, while the latter needs both good equipment documentation (e.g., schematics, wiring diagrams) and detailed knowledge and reasoning ability on the part of the ATSS personnel.

The overarching goal of ATSS personnel is to maximize the availability of equipment and facilities in good working order in the NAS by performing these two functions—scheduled activities and corrective maintenance (FAA, 2011a).[3] Minimizing failures and reducing the time to repair and certify equipment are high priorities because equipment failure prevents achievement of this goal.

Scheduled preventive maintenance reduces the probability of equipment failure. Presumably there is an optimal amount of preventive maintenance that, for a given total staffing cost, will minimize down time or, conversely, maximize availability. The timing of most equipment failure cannot be anticipated with certainty. When extensive historical reliability data such as "mean time between failures" exist, some general predictions about the time frames for failure may be possible. Because the personnel who conduct the scheduled preventive maintenance are likely to be the same staff who respond to unanticipated failures, corrective maintenance can often be addressed at the same time as an unanticipated failure. However, the extent to which the preventive and corrective maintenance occur together requires further examination.

Discipline Types and Staff Substitutions

ATSS work requires expertise in specialties including electromechanical environmental control systems, power generation, automation, and electronics maintenance. As a result, most ATSS personnel specialize in one or more of the five recognized disciplines in the series explained in the following quotations from the FAA National Airspace Capital Investment Plan (FAA, 2011b) and from a recent job posting on the Electronic Technicians Association website:

> **Communication:** "Communication between pilots and controllers is an essential element of air traffic control. Pilots and controllers normally use [VHF/UHF] radios for communication, and because en route control sectors cover areas that extend beyond direct radio range, remotely located radio sites are used to provide extended coverage. The controller activates radios at these sites and ground telecommunication lines carry the information exchange to and from air traffic control facilities. If ground links are not available, communication satellite links can be used to connect pilots with controllers. Backup systems are always available to provide continued ability to maintain communications when the primary systems fail." (FAA, 2011b:43)

> **Surveillance:** "To provide separation services to aircraft, air traffic controllers must have an accurate display of all aircraft under their control. Controller displays use a variety of inputs, including radar and transponder information, to show the location of aircraft. Surveillance data are provided by the following technologies: Primary radar—The radar beam is reflected off the aircraft back to the radar receiver; Secondary radar—A reply is generated by the aircraft transponder back to the radar in response to a radar signal; Multi-lateration—Multiple ground sensors receive aircraft transponder signals allowing triangulation for position; and Automatic Dependent Surveillance Broadcast—Aircraft determines its location using GPS and broadcasts that information. Automation systems process radar data and other inputs and send it to the displays. En route facilities use the Air Route Surveillance Radar (ARSR), and

[3]Mike Perrone, president, Professional Aviation Safety Specialists, AFL-CIO, presentation to the Committee on Staffing Needs of Systems Specialists in Aviation, December 6, 2012.

terminal facilities use Airport Surveillance Radar (ASR) as primary radars. The ARSR and ASR radars are primary because they do not require a cooperative transmission from an aircraft to detect and track its location. En route and terminal facilities normally use secondary radars called the Air Traffic Control Beacon Interrogators (ATCBI) and Mode Select (Mode S) for traffic separation. Secondary radar sends a signal to aircraft equipped with a transponder. The transponder sends a reply, which can be processed to determine the aircraft call sign, altitude, speed, and its position. Using ATCBI or Mode S enhances the controller's ability to separate traffic because flight and altitude information supplement the position display for each aircraft." (FAA, 2011b:49)

Navaid: "There are two major types of navigational aids: those used for en route navigation, and those used for precision approach and landing guidance. The en route aids have traditionally been radio transmitters that provide pilots direction and/or distance from their location. The ground based system commonly used for en route navigation is the Very High Frequency Omnidirectional Range with Distance Measuring Equipment (VOR with DME). There are more than 1,000 VORs spread across the United States. They enable pilots to determine an accurate position and also define the Victor and Jet airways, which are published routes based on straight lines from VOR to VOR. Airways simplify route planning and provide predictability for air traffic controllers who often must project an aircraft's future position to avoid conflicts. Pilots use VOR/DME to follow their planned routes accurately under all visibility conditions" (FAA, 2011b:54). . . .

"Precision landing guidance systems and associated equipment support low-visibility operations by providing radio signals and approach lights to help pilots land safely in limited visibility. The current most widely-used precision landing aids are Instrument Landing Systems (ILS) that guide pilots to runway ends using a pair of radio beams—one for lateral guidance and the other for vertical guidance—to define the approach glidepath—so that pilots can follow it to the runway using cockpit instrumentation. There are more than 1,200 ILSs installed in the United States." (FAA, 2011b:54)

Automation: "Automation is a core element of the air traffic control system. Controllers require a real-time display of aircraft location as well as information about the operating characteristics of aircraft they are tracking—such as speed and altitude—to keep the approximately 50,000 flights safely separated every day. Automation gives controllers continuously updated displays of aircraft position, identification, speed, and altitude as well as whether the aircraft is level, climbing, or descending. Automation systems can also continue to show an aircraft's track when there is a temporary loss of surveillance information. It does this by calculating an aircraft's ground speed and then uses it to project an aircraft's future position." (FAA, 2011b:36)

Environmental: ATSS work on power generation on airfield and ARTCC and TRACON facilities, and lights used for landing aircraft. Primary responsibilities relate to "the installation, maintenance, modification and certification of ENVIRONMENTAL and lighted navigational aids systems and services such as: Precision approach Path Indicator, Visual Approach Slope Indicator, Approach Lighting System with Sequenced Flashing Lights, Runway End Identification Lights, Runway Status Lights, Engine Generators, transfer switches, heating ventilating and air conditioning, and knowledge of the national electric code." (Electronic Technicians Association, 2013)

Although safe and effective operation of the NAS requires staffing in all of the above disciplines nationwide, the type of organization in which an ATSS works affects the specific skills required of that individual ATSS.[4] Although the ATSS job description is broad-based, in actual practice individuals may operate within the primary discipline of their work site, even if the member has multiple certifications. When developing a staffing model to describe required staff size or allocating staff, care should be taken

[4]Rich McCormick, director, Labor Analysis, FAA. ATSS Briefing for the National Academy of Sciences. Presentation to the Committee on Staffing Needs of Systems Specialists in Aviation, October 19, 2012.

TABLE 2-1 Percentage of 2101 Disciplines Represented by Location

Discipline	2101 Code	ARTCC	TRACON	Core	GNAS	SOC/OCC[a]
Automation	Auto	34	26	0	0	0
Communications	Comm	28	21	1	0	0
Environmental	Env	30	33	19	1	0
Navigational Aid	Nav	0	0	4	1	0
Radar	Rad	0	0	11	2	0
Multi-discipline (2)	M2	4	16	46	7	0
Multi-discipline (3)	M3	3	4	10	5	0
Multi-discipline (4 or 5)	M4	1	0	8	84	0
Unknown		0	0	0	0	100
Total Percentage		100	100	100	100	100

[a]The SOC/OCC disciplines are shown as 100 percent unknown because a recent personnel survey has not been conducted for the SOCs/OCCs.
SOURCE: FAA Data Extract from existing FAA information management systems, Rich McCormick, director, Labor Analysis, FAA. January 18, 2013. This is a snapshot of actual discipline distribution in a given past point in time; it does not necessarily reflect the required discipline distribution.

not to automatically assume that any ATSS employee is skilled across most or all disciplines. According to the information provided to the committee, specialization and work in a particular discipline are more common in the ARTCCs and TRACON facilities. ATSS personnel assigned to Core Airports and GNAS facilities tend to be skilled in two or more disciplines.[5] Thus, a valid model should determine ATSS needs by skill area at each location and work site. In some locations, there may be value in considering multi-disciplined staffing, particularly in smaller work sites. The committee recognized very early in its study that ATSS job incumbents (even experienced, expert ATSS personnel) are clearly not interchangeable commodities and therefore cannot not be treated in that manner in a staffing model.

Equipment integral to the NAS can only be certified by ATSS technicians who are trained and certified to work on that equipment. Because of certification requirements, ATSS personnel are not interchangeable. In practice, however, especially in small, understaffed, or remote locations, an available or conveniently located ATSS employee may perform maintenance work under the direction of a certified technician, and the work will be certified when the certified ATSS employee is available. Table 2-1 shows how ATSS personnel are distributed across disciplines and facilities. The table also indicates the percentage of ATSS personnel who are able to work in multiple disciplines.

Many Technical Operations work sites are organized and staffed by facility function and discipline. For example, ATSS personnel in SSCs serving TRACON facilities and ARTCCs maintain equipment that is associated with the particular facility and almost entirely housed within the compound of that facility. However, both TRACON facilities and ARTCCs depend on pieces of equipment in remote areas—outside the compounds of major facilities—that must be maintained. Because the number of individual pieces of equipment that are located outside of the TRACON and ARTCC facilities is small, ATSS personnel are not typically assigned to those remote locations for reasons of economy. Instead,

[5]In Table 2-1, note the specialization and depth at the ARTCC and TRACON locations as compared to use of more multi-discipline personnel at the Core Airports and GNAS locations.

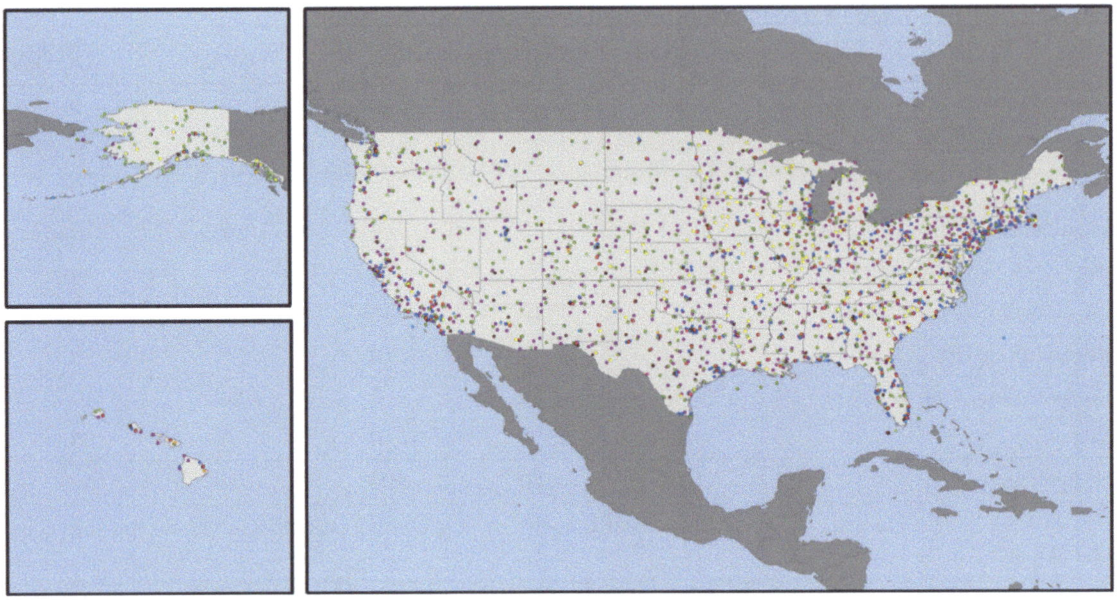

FIGURE 2-2 A mapping of 8,505 of the 66,749 facilities and equipment locations across the NAS.
SOURCE: Department of Transportation, 2012.

staff in the GNAS and other work sites must travel to these locations to provide maintenance. Thus, unlike a TRACON facility or ARTCC, the GNAS offices may serve as a location from which ATSS personnel stage their work and may not have on-site NAS facilities or equipment. Approximately 2,800 members of the 2101-series are assigned to 190 GNAS offices.[6] Typically, ATSS personnel assigned to a Core Airport work on the grounds of that airport; however, some equipment (e.g., radar) may be located short distances from the airport grounds. Similarly, ATSS personnel assigned to a SOC/OCC usually work on that property. Figure 2-2 illustrates the nationwide distribution of NAS equipment and indicates the relative concentration of equipment requiring service.

Beyond the need for certified personnel (by discipline, by work area, and by geographic area), staffing the ATSS job series is complicated by the difficulty of planning the work itself. While there are very predictable factors associated with the work requirements for any one ATSS employee at a given location (for example, preventive maintenance schedules are well-defined), there are also events that occur unpredictably (for example, corrective maintenance required by equipment failure). Further complicating the planning task is the need to maintain required standards, so local management establishes "watch" schedules to ensure the availability of appropriately qualified staff at all required times.[7] The committee understands that there are limited reliable data available that address the relative time spent (again, by discipline and by work area) between these types of tasks (i.e., preventive and corrective maintenance). Thus, planning for ATSS time cannot currently be based on accurate records of past activities.

[6]Personal communication from Rich McCormick, director, Labor Analysis, FAA, to staff, January 18, 2013. Subject line: "Tech Ops Headcount."

[7]Mike Perrone, president, Professional Aviation Safety Specialists, AFL-CIO, presentation to the Committee on Staffing Needs of Systems Specialists in Aviation, December 6, 2012.

Evolving Systems and Services

ATSS personnel currently maintain a wide array of equipment and are likely to do so for a considerable time to come. The FAA is continually upgrading equipment to facilitate efficiency and safety of the airways as well as to reduce maintenance requirements, and ATSS personnel have to work effectively with the new or reconfigured equipment and with the older equipment that remains in place. In many instances, the changes in equipment are aimed at increasing system reliability. Over time, software has increased in importance, changing the skill set needed by ATSS personnel but also allowing, for example, more remote control or reconfiguration of equipment (GAO, 2010).

The FAA's Next Generation (NextGen) expects to overhaul the NAS comprehensively, based on a series of continual improvements and upgrades.[8] As equipment improvements are being made, the FAA also plans to decommission obsolete or nonfunctioning equipment. In order to properly model the ATSS workload and tasks, accurate information is needed about which systems are active, which will no longer be required, and which will be added.[9] In addition, the time frames for new installations and decommissioning will be required. Although the committee received briefing and information on NextGen, it was not given the actual schedules for installing new equipment and decommissioning older equipment and was not able to conclusively reflect on the specific details of NextGen and their implications for ATSS staffing. However, for the purposes of this report, the point is not the precise schedule for NextGen transitions but rather the importance of taking into account changes to the NAS components and their impact on staffing needs in future models. In regard to a decommissioning policy, the committee was told that Technical Operations is working toward developing a more comprehensive document that will address a national decommissioning process.[10]

One outcome of the NextGen implementation could be an eventual decrease in the workload for ATSS personnel overall because there will be fewer ground-based systems to maintain and the replacement systems are expected to have higher reliability than current systems. However, legacy systems will remain as critical elements of the NAS during the transition and beyond.[11] For example, some radar systems are likely to be maintained for national security reasons as backup in the event of satellite failure. As a result, it is highly likely that the workload demands on ATSS personnel will increase (thus increasing the staffing requirements) for some period of time until the removal of the legacy equipment offsets the demands of the new systems (GAO, 2010). Considering all of these factors, the committee believes that challenges will exist in staffing individual locations with the right mix of certified personnel in the proper disciplines, even if a perfect staffing model for the ATSS job series as a whole could be created.

---

[8]Steve Bradford, chief scientist, Architecture & NextGen Development, FAA, presentation on the Next Generation Air Traffic Management System to the Committee on Staffing Needs of Systems Specialists in Aviation, December 6, 2012.

[9]Dynamic, up-to-date lists of equipment, facilities, and services can be vital ingredients in modeling the current workforce requirement. The out-year estimates or timelines for adding, removing, or modifying within the system are vital for prediction of out-year workforce requirements. In the Air Force, when major systems acquisitions are to be added to the inventory, an official Manpower Estimate Report is mandated as part of the process, and this report can be a basis for out-year budgeting of manpower (U.S. Air Force, 2011). Similar estimates or modules to be added to a staffing model could help the FAA predict future needs.

[10]Personal communication from Rich McCormick to committee staff, March 22, 2013, regarding decommissioning.

[11]Steve Bradford, chief scientist, Architecture & NextGen Development, FAA, presentation on the Next Generation Air Traffic Management System to the Committee on Staffing Needs of Systems Specialists in Aviation, December 6, 2012.

ACKNOWLEDGED PROBLEM AREAS IN THE ATSS WORK ENVIRONMENT

Throughout the data-gathering process, multiple stakeholder representatives expressed some consistent concerns that the committee agrees are problem areas within the ATSS work environment. These problem areas need to be addressed in whatever staffing model is developed.

First, current staffing levels are not optimal at all locations and in all disciplines. That is, the overall staffing level for ATSS of 6,100, which is specified in the collective bargaining agreement between the FAA and the Professional Aviation Safety Specialists (PASS) represents a negotiated compromise (GAO, 2010; Professional Airways Systems Specialists, 2000). Even if this were an optimal total number, there is some level of consensus between staff and management that the distribution of ATSS personnel by discipline and by work area needs to be improved.

Second, there seems to be agreement among FAA management and ATSS personnel that the process in place for hiring, training, and certifying new ATSS personnel is not optimal. In many instances, Technical Operations will hire a new employee and will then have to request a sufficient quota through the "annual call for training" to train that employee at the centralized facility. The training branch may not have budgeted for the additional training classes or have space for an additional student. If the training slot is not granted, then the employee has to wait for space to become available, which can take many months. After returning from training, there are also issues with availability of appropriate staff to conduct required on-the-job training (OJT) that leads to certification because it may be difficult to take a journeyman technician away from assigned work on the NAS to complete the new employee's training. Some ATSS personnel are frustrated by the requirement to train new employees if limited staffing levels require that they delay their NAS-related work.[12]

A third problem area is that, because new hires may require 4 to 18 months to become certified in a single discipline, these new hires will not be one-for-one substitutes for certified staff and will not be able to contribute as much to accomplishing the maintenance workload as certified staff. Although noncertified ATSS personnel can work on certain components to alleviate some of the workload pressures of those who are certified, before the equipment returns to service a certified specialist must review the work performed and certify the equipment. The committee was told that there is an ongoing effort to adjust the hiring system to address these training delays (i.e., planning for even-flow hiring), which should address the need to have a scheduled flow of new employees into the NAS maintenance system. Nevertheless, the committee remains concerned that this adjustment does not address the need to have adequate specialized training classes on the equipment requiring certification. Reliance on a manual system referred to as the "annual call" impairs the ability of the agency to be adequately prepared to train the right number of people in the appropriate training classes, specifically those requiring certification.[13] Thus, it appears that certain human-systems integration (HSI) domains such as Personnel and Training (U.S. Air Force, undated) represent concurrent challenges that require continued exploration and analysis, even as the FAA seeks to create a robust ATSS manpower model.

The varying travel and environmental issues specific to NAS locations represent additional factors that the committee consistently heard identified as complicating the development of a staffing model. For example, ATSS personnel at some locations are required to maintain equipment that is located a significant distance from their typical work location,[14] although, to minimize the overall impact of travel

---

[12]Comments submitted to the Staffing Needs of Systems Specialists in Aviation Stakeholder webpage, 2013.

[13]Vaughn Turner, vice president, Technical Operations, FAA, comment to the Committee on Staffing Needs of Systems Specialists in Aviation, January 24, 2013.

[14]Mike Perrone, president, PASS, AFL-CIO, presentation to the Committee on Staffing Needs of Systems Specialists in Aviation, December 6, 2012.

time, ATSS personnel try to plan their remote visits to perform several tasks in one trip to the remote site. In addition to distance, there are specific accessibility issues present for some ATSS tasks at some locations. For example, the equipment may be located in an area that is not convenient to major roads or in an area that requires travel through hazardous terrain or severe inclement weather. In an extreme example, a piece of equipment located on a mountain top in winter can require several days of snow clearance to provide ATSS access to even begin the required task (Grant Thornton, 2012). Where travel and environmental challenges are significant, they should be documented and considered in tailoring features of a model.

Needs Identified by ATSS Stakeholders

ATSS job incumbents served as one major source of information for the committee. The committee gathered this information through presentations by representatives from the FAA and PASS, through visits to ATSS job sites, and through stakeholder comments posted by ATSS personnel on a webpage the committee established for this purpose. The committee's summary of ATSS stakeholder perspectives is categorized around the following issues:

- Training issues
- Training impacts on workload
- Watch schedules and shift assignments
- Equipment issues
- Other issues

Training Issues

Training progression for an ATSS is not a continuous, uninterrupted process that leads to certification in a predictable fashion, in part because staffing levels play a major role in the availability of a technician (and the relevant supervisory personnel) to be released for resident training at the Mike Monroney Aeronautical Center in Oklahoma City. Thus, supervisors and technicians must balance training goals with workload assignments. Furthermore, student quotas for resident classes are driven by the training academy's budget, so availability and access are limited.[15] For example, an ATSS trainee may have to wait months for a resident training slot (itself potentially lasting many months). This resident training is required before the OJT, which leads to eventual certification, can commence. Further, in most cases, resident training is not completed in one contiguous block of time; an ATSS trainee may have to make multiple trips to Oklahoma City to complete a sequence of courses.[16] However, if the trainee's primary duties have priority and substitute personnel are unavailable, a return to training can be put on hold for many months. Other forms of training, including equipment manufacturer training, computer-based instruction, and online training, also take technicians away from their primary duties in maintaining and repairing the equipment in the NAS.[17]

Nontechnical training requirements also limit the availability of ATSS trainees. Nontechnical training includes security training, training involving human resources requirements, and required safety training. This safety training involves topics such as electrical safety, climbing, working in confined spaces, hazardous materials, and more. In addition, nontechnical training can include mandated training in equal

[15]Comments submitted to Staffing Needs of Systems Specialists in Aviation Stakeholder webpage, 2013.
[16]Ibid.
[17]Ibid.

employment opportunity or other training that may be related to the introduction of a new agency policy or a change in an existing policy. This type of training is generally directed from the headquarters level with a high priority and short deadlines for completion.[18]

Training Impacts on Workload

Many of the skills that ATSS personnel require are acquired by formal OJT or by shadowing certified staffing specialists. When a new technician returns from training, establishing an effective relationship between a journeyman technician and the new technician to complete OJT and the certification process is a critical task. Although some journeymen embrace the opportunity to teach new hires and make an effort to provide good training and mentorship, others see it as an unwelcome addition to their workload. The latter attitude could lead to less than effective OJT for some technicians.

Staffing levels may also prevent an effective mentorship between experienced technicians and newly trained technicians because the journeyman might not have time to provide OJT. Technicians do receive training to qualify as OJT instructors; however, this training falls short of what is needed to become good trainers and mentors for the new employees.[19] Finally, although an ATSS may complete training assignments and be certified—a process that can take 3 to 5 years[20]—this journeyman level of proficiency is not a substitute for the skills of veteran workers. Until technicians have developed extensive on-the-job experience, their work requires a relatively high level of supervision and oversight.[21] That is, until a trainee technician is certified, that technician cannot independently maintain, restore to service, or certify elements of the NAS (tasks that are the highest priorities for ATSS personnel), even though the trainee is being counted as one of the staff assigned to the facility.

In addition, the time a journeyman technician uses to provide formal OJT or proctor certification exams for technicians-in-training can conflict with higher priority work on NAS equipment. This conflict delays both completion of training and certification of the new employee, as well as scheduled preventive maintenance.[22] Thus, the training phase affects workload in two ways: by decreasing the effective number of certified technicians at a facility and by increasing the workload of certified technicians who maintain the NAS.

Watch Schedules and Shift Assignments

For each of its facilities, the FAA provides guidance on the number and type of ATSS employees required on each shift throughout the day. This number could change on an hourly basis, depending on the amount of air traffic expected. This *coverage requirement* then guides the formulation of the basic watch schedule, which shows the weekdays and daily hours when coverage is required and also includes provisions for shift rotations as well as employees' regular days off.[23] The FAA has conducted risk assessments of some facilities to determine how to utilize the available employees most effectively.

[18]Mike Perrone, president, PASS, AFL-CIO, presentation to the Committee on Staffing Needs of Systems Specialists in Aviation, December 6, 2012.

[19]Comments submitted to Staffing Needs of Systems Specialists in Aviation Stakeholder webpage, 2013.

[20]Mike Perrone, president, PASS, AFL-CIO, presentation to the Committee on Staffing Needs of Systems Specialists in Aviation, December 6, 2012.

[21]Comments submitted to Staffing Needs of Systems Specialists in Aviation Stakeholder webpage, 2013.

[22]Ibid.

[23]Mike Perrone, president, PASS, AFL-CIO, presentation to the Committee on Staffing Needs of Systems Specialists in Aviation, December 6, 2012.

However, these risk assessments only address the impact to the NAS if a facility or service becomes inoperable and there is insufficient staffing to immediately respond. They do not change the magnitude or nature of the work required to restore service. In risk assessment terms, if the inoperable facility can be backed up by a nearby facility, then the repair response can be effectively delayed and the impact to the NAS is minimal. Based partly on these assessments, watch schedules frequently change to provide coverage of inadequately staffed facilities.[24]

A risk assessment is completed with many factors being considered, including hours of operation of the airport and surrounding needs of the user. In addition, they are always completed in conjunction with the Air Traffic Operations personnel who are the most familiar with equipment usage and system demands (FAA, 2011a). For example, although a small facility in an area with other facilities nearby may be most effectively served by coverage around the clock, every day (24/7), a risk assessment could conclude that a maintenance problem would not significantly affect the NAS because of redundancy in the nearby systems. The FAA might then reduce the coverage to 16 hours a day with call-back responsibilities. Thus, for 8 hours of each day, there will be minimal or no staff at the facility and employees would need to be called in for emergencies. Some stakeholders believe that this policy focuses too strongly on efficiency while potentially undermining effectiveness.[25]

Equipment Issues

Because of the varied equipment inventory of the NAS (e.g., communications, navigation, surveillance, environmental, and automation equipment), a typical ATSS employee may be responsible for three or more highly complex systems. Currently, it is common for an ATSS to be expected to be a "jack of all trades"—that is, a technician who is able to respond to equipment needs across multiple systems.[26] This issue was affirmed by comments submitted in the stakeholder feedback.[27] Management in each individual service area must consider the diversity and complexity of the equipment inventory and have the necessary numbers of ATSS personnel with the required training and skills to respond to the maintenance and repair needs in that area.

Upgrades, equipment changes, and reconfigurations of existing equipment are frequent and typically involve both hardware and software changes, resulting in new skill requirements for ATSS personnel, particularly in the use of software to maintain and reconfigure equipment. Because ATSS employees are the sole personnel authorized to certify and maintain the NAS and its components (including installing, testing, troubleshooting, repairing, and certifying all radar, communications, navigational aids, airport lighting, and backup power systems), realizing value from the approximately $20 billion per year investment in the FAA hinges significantly on this group of technicians.

The committee also noted that the demands of training and equipment modifications are interrelated. When equipment is updated or replaced, technicians must acquire the skills through training on the new equipment. For example, updates to the Critical and Essential Power System at an ARTCC will require every Environmental Support Unit (ESU) technician at that facility to attend training in Oklahoma City. The absence of one technician for the several weeks required to complete this training could significantly affect the staffing levels and watch coverage requirement. Thus, facilities that are already understaffed may not be able to staff coverage requirements during periods of intensive training on new equipment.

---

[24]Ibid.

[25]Ibid.

[26]Mike Perrone, president, PASS, AFL-CIO, presentation to the Committee on Staffing Needs of Systems Specialists in Aviation, December 6, 2012.

[27]Comments submitted to Staffing Needs of Systems Specialists in Aviation Stakeholder webpage, 2013.

Other Issues That Impact the Workload and Staffing of ATSS Personnel

Safety protocols place additional constraints on ATSS personnel workload and their availability. FAA technical manuals often direct that, for safety reasons, tasks may not be performed without at least two ATSS personnel being present.[28] Working on high-voltage equipment, climbing on ladders, travel to remote sites under hazardous weather conditions, and rotating shifts at high-impact facilities that are staffed around the clock are all tasks that require multiple technicians. For example, ESU technicians work on mechanical and electrical equipment (e.g., batteries, chillers, generators) that require two technicians for safety reasons. In addition to the regular preventive maintenance on that equipment, ESU technicians must be available to restore the Critical Power Distribution System without delay if it goes down.[29] Although in theory 7 ESU technicians could staff a facility with 24/7 coverage requirements, the added requirement that 2 technicians must work on some equipment increases the required minimum number of staff in that discipline to 14, if certified managers are not available to work in situations requiring two workers.

Travel time to remote facilities, which can be up to 200 miles distant, can further limit the availability of a technician to perform scheduled maintenance and potentially increase the time a system remains out of service. Technicians are dispatched from an SSC to remote sites, so managers and technicians must manage travel time along with scheduling the work itself. The committee was told that overnight travel for preventive maintenance might not be budgeted, so when ATSS personnel travel to a remote location that is several hours away, they must return to their home facility at the end of each day and drive multiple times to the location to finish the maintenance depending on the manager's discretion with the budget. Consistently providing a budget for hotel and meal costs could allow the preventive maintenance to be completed more quickly and allow more tasks to be completed because less time would be spent driving.[30] When the budget or the staffing does not allow for either of these options, then the efficiency and effectiveness of maintenance of the NAS could be compromised.

Leaves of absence also limit the availability of ATSS personnel. Some examples include family medical leave or service in the military reserves, which can leave facilities with significant staffing shortages for long periods of time. A number of ATSS personnel serve in the military reserves and are called on to fulfill commitments ranging from weekend service to long-term deployment, although the number of ATSS personnel who have military obligations and the timing of those obligations is not always known.[31] The committee learned that, although the FAA did not know the total number of ATSS personnel serving in the military reserves, it does know the number who have taken leave to serve. While commitment of ATSS personnel to military service should be commended, management at facilities will have some uncertainty in planning schedules, given this lack of knowledge about the number, duration, and timing of these commitments and the unpredictability of current and future military conflicts.

Many other factors have an effect on workload. Many are small, but in aggregate they create significant demands on the ATSS workload. One such factor affecting availability is worker fatigue. For example, if a technician were to work excessive amounts of overtime, that individual might experience chronic fatigue to a level that would jeopardize effectiveness and safety. It is always wise to thoroughly explore and understand the use of overtime, a possible contributing factor to fatigue, when assessing

[28]Ibid.

[29]Ibid.

[30]Mike Perrone, president, PASS, AFL-CIO, presentation to the Committee on Staffing Needs of Systems Specialists in Aviation, December 6, 2012.

[31]Personal communication on numbers of personnel in the military reserves from Rich McCormick to the Committee on Staffing Needs of Systems Specialists in Aviation, February 12, 2013.

required staffing levels. Article 47 of the current PASS/FAA labor agreement discusses overtime rules and considerations. In response to a committee request for data on overtime, the FAA provided data on the use of ATSS overtime during fiscal year 2012. It showed that only 15 percent of ATSS personnel had no overtime in the year, 50 percent used less than 50 hours, 20 percent used between 50 and 100 hours, and 3 percent had greater than 250 hours of overtime in that year.[32] Continued analyses of documented/undocumented overtime should be undertaken, usually during the familiarization phase of a model effort (see Chapter 3), and it should be monitored after model implementation. The FAA provided a management plan to mitigate fatigue and its consequent hazards (FAA, 2012b). Although making and enforcing rules increases the safety of the workers and of the NAS, those actions potentially reduce the available technician resource. A related factor is the effect that frustrating and annoying circumstances may have on ATSS personnel and their morale and stress levels. These factors in turn affect other factors that may have a significant effect on workload. For example, to the extent that morale has an impact on turnover, a chain of events starting with inability to get training when needed could result in higher turnover. Another of these factors is administrative tasks; the committee found that a technician's workload can be increased by the need to respond to ad hoc requests for such things as spare parts inventories, vehicle surveys, etc.[33]

Needs Identified by Other Stakeholders

The committee found that there are multiple stakeholders with an interest in ATSS staffing. To ensure that the committee had an opportunity to consider the views of stakeholders, the National Research Council established a webpage that allowed for comments as well as an opportunity to upload longer documents relating to one or more of four subject areas: *Equipment*, *Training*, *Workload*, and *Models*. In addition, respondents could choose *None of the Above*. Although the committee does not know the exact participation rate for the comments, the primary stakeholders (see Table 1-1) were contacted and asked to advertise the comments webpage to their constituents. The webpage did not require the respondents to include their job title, but most indicated that they worked for the FAA or a specific Technical Operations facility. The committee received 168 responses through this webpage for stakeholder input, the vast majority of which were posted by ATSS employees. By subject area, the leading issue was *Workload* (138) followed by *Training* (99), *Equipment* (76), and *Models* (21). The committee's inspection and interpretation of the associated written comments yielded a broadly similar emphasis—*Insufficient Staffing Level* (93), *Training Issues* (21), *Poor Staffing Distribution* (8), *Appropriate Staffing Level* (7), and *Miscellany* (19). The broad themes of comments in the *Insufficient Staffing Level* designation included a perceived high manager-to-technician ratio and weaknesses of the staffing methods based upon allocation per facility, but the dominant issue was excessive workload demands. Comments designated as *Appropriate Staffing Level* generally expressed present satisfaction but included concerns for the future, given as yet unspecified new demands from NextGen, as well as sequestration cutbacks. The *Miscellany* comments ranged from suggested best practices to skepticism about the National Research Council's study process.[34]

[32]Personal communication on ATSS overtime from Rich McCormick to the Committee on Staffing Needs of Systems Specialists in Aviation, January 2013.

[33]Mike Perrone, president, PASS, AFL-CIO, presentation to the Committee on Staffing Needs of Systems Specialists in Aviation, December 6, 2012.

[34]Comments submitted to Staffing Needs of Systems Specialists in Aviation Stakeholder webpage, 2013.

MAJOR DRIVERS BEHIND ATSS STAFFING NEEDS

The Next Generation Air Transportation System

The FAA currently employs slightly fewer than 6,100 ATSS personnel, who are responsible for approximately 65,000 individual facilities and equipment that collectively define the NAS (Department of Transportation, 2012; FAA, 2012c). The principal driver behind ATSS staffing has been the need to maintain or oversee an extensive system of ground-based navigational, communications, environmental, and surveillance equipment. Although the largely satellite-based NextGen opens the possibility, at least in concept, of significantly reducing the existing inventory of ground-based navigation aids (e.g., Non-Directional Beacon and Very High Frequency Omnidirectional Range [VOR]), the FAA has concluded that a reduced VOR-based navigation network will be required for the indefinite future in the event of failure of the Global Navigation Satellite System (GNSS) (FAA, 2012d). This VOR Minimum Operational Network (MON) would comprise approximately half of the existing 967 stations, with virtually no reductions in the western United States (FAA, 2012e). The MON will support non-GNSS guidance to within 100 nautical miles of airports with Instrument Landing Systems or VOR approach procedures. This network reduction, planned for completion by 2020, will be accomplished through a combination of programmed decommissioning and nonrepair of failed units.[35] The continental U.S. Non-Directional Beacon network is currently being reduced through attrition (Department of Commerce, 2008), with its functionality compensated in part by GNSS-based approach procedures. As NextGen is not expected to significantly decrease the current role of ATSS personnel across all disciplines, and it could increase the complexity of some job tasks (GAO, 2010), the key question in anticipating ATSS staffing levels to the year 2020 and beyond is the degree to which the decreased work demand from the reduction by half of the VOR network will be offset or exceeded by the new demands of NextGen. In this regard, the committee notes that no VOR reductions are currently planned for the Western U.S. Mountainous Area (FAA, 2012e) where, in general, the least accessible VORs (e.g., on snowy mountaintops rather than adjacent to runways) are located. Furthermore, the MON will continue to be NAS reportable, and thus failure within the system will require immediate response by ATSS personnel.

As the FAA transitions to NextGen, decisions will be made on how to redeploy and potentially eliminate staff associated with obsolete systems. The committee emphasizes that such planning is intrinsically risky, as unproven technology can thwart even the most judicious prognosticator. A relevant example of such unintended consequences arose when rollout of the En Route Automation Modernization system was delayed by four years, during which time the FAA reduced resources and eliminated training on the legacy equipment that the new system was replacing (GAO, 2012). Lastly, the FAA has not yet publicly specified its comprehensive maintenance requirements for NextGen equipment. An effective staffing model should go beyond documenting today's required ATSS staffing levels; instead, a robust and accessible staffing model should be capable of incorporating such additional inputs as they become available, not only with respect to NextGen but also with respect to inevitable continuing technological advances.

Finding 2-1: Changes to the NAS such as NextGen and MON implementation and unspecified decommissioning policies all make the amount of work to be performed by ATSS personnel ambiguous and complicate the FAA's task in developing an appropriate staffing model for ATSS.

---

[35]Vaughn Turner, vice president, Technical Operations, FAA, comment to the Committee on Staffing Needs of Systems Specialists in Aviation, January 24, 2013.

Conclusion 2-1: Developing and using a successful staffing model to predict future outcomes will be limited by unknowns such as decommissioning policies for legacy equipment, installation of NextGen equipment, and consolidation of facilities.

Recommendation 2-1: The FAA should ensure that ATSS staffing models will incorporate new information about the unknown factors that affect ATSS staffing such as NextGen as it becomes available, consider their staffing implications, and use appropriate modeling techniques to plan for contingencies.

Aging Workforce and Succession Planning

A critical potential instability in secure maintenance of the NAS is the large number of ATSS personnel who are at or nearing retirement eligibility.[36] In a 2010 report, the GAO found that 23 percent of ATSS personnel would be eligible for retirement by 2012, 31 percent by 2015, and more than 50 percent by 2020. Extrapolating from recent retirements, they estimated that the FAA could face more than 500 retirements in fiscal year (FY) 2015 and about 900 in FY 2020 (GAO, 2010). Although not all the ATSS personnel eligible to retire are likely to do so in the year they become eligible (and there is no mandatory retirement age; FAA, 2012f), this potential instability in staff has been exacerbated by the limitations imposed by the 6,100 ATSS staffing agreement. Because it is sometimes interpreted (erroneously) as a ceiling on personnel numbers, this policy has had the effect of severely limiting succession planning. For example, intensive recruitment of ATSS staff at the end of the FY is typically driven by recent separations without accounting for the many years it takes to train and certify new technicians.[37] Both PASS and FAA officials acknowledged the nonoptimal consequences of this practice, and the recently implemented even-flow hiring policy[38] may perform significantly better at matching employee recruitment and hiring to both current and future facility needs. The challenge of modeling future staffing needs while maintaining and certifying the legacy equipment will continue until the phases of NextGen implementation are known.

External Influences

The general trend toward outsourcing services that has influenced FAA staffing in several areas (e.g., contract towers) appears unlikely to impact ATSS staffing levels significantly because maintenance of the NAS has been considered an "inherently governmental function," which means it must be conducted by government employees and not contractors (Office of Management and Budget, 2003).[39]

The committee heard concerns expressed from both FAA management and technician representatives that maintaining ATSS staffing levels in high cost-of-living regions is a constant challenge. Although federal employment policies provide for a cost-of-living pay differential in high-cost areas, experience indicates that the additional remuneration is not preventing a high rate of turnover in some areas. Furthermore, the policy of permitting ATSS personnel to request transfers at any time during their assignment (even allowing ATSS personnel to submit transfer requests on their first day at a location) is a

[36]The committee believes that attrition/accession models are best handled as separate human resource algorithms based upon the staffing model targets.

[37]Comments submitted to Staffing Needs of Systems Specialists in Aviation Stakeholder webpage, 2013.

[38]Vaughn Turner, vice president, Technical Operations, FAA, comment to the Committee on Staffing Needs of Systems Specialists in Aviation, January 24, 2013.

[39]See discussion in Chapter 1.

continuing source of frustration to planning staffing allocation levels—particularly in high-cost areas.[40] Facilities in these areas sometimes pay for the technician's training with the assumption that the new hire will progress through certification and remain on staff, only to have the technician request a transfer to a lower cost-of-living area as soon as training is completed. Although understandable, this practice negatively affects management's ability to schedule watch coverage over the long term. For example, when a technician who has just completed certification requests a transfer and leaves the facility, the next technician hired will have to undergo the training and certification process before being able to work on the NAS without supervision, which could result in months of understaffing for the facility and additional work for management and ATSS personnel.

Internal Influences

Consolidation of Facilities

The FAA has in some cases realized efficiencies and workplace synergies from collocating geographically separated facilities (e.g., the Southern California TRACON). In concert with NextGen, future infrastructure improvements are aimed at consolidation of existing facilities into purpose-designed, state-of-the-art complexes. For example, the planned New York Integrated Control Facility[41] would combine both Terminal and En Route facilities that are currently controlled separately from the New York TRACON in Suffolk County and the New York ARTCC in Nassau County, both on Long Island. One consideration in choosing a site for relocation is available and inexpensive land, such as an exurban or semirural site, to both minimize facility costs and provide an affordable environment for employees. Although locating the new consolidated facility in either Nassau or Suffolk Counties might be expected to cause minor dislocations to the technician staff, locating it to another location off Long Island may, in the near and intermediate term, be substantially disruptive to the existing workforce and could stimulate numerous staff relocations. Thus, an attempt to realize this sort of long-term cost savings needs to be managed in a manner that minimizes alienation of ATSS staff, possibly by providing transitions staged in discrete steps over several years.

New and Continuing Knowledge Demands

In individual discussions with ATSS personnel, some specialists reported that access to relevant programs that extend or diversify their ability to become certified in multiple equipment types within the NAS were limited by training quotas and travel budget shortfalls. These delays make it more difficult to complete training progression programs. Also noted was that some training classes were not at a sufficiently high technical level to be useful in the field. For example, a course might consist primarily of equipment overviews, rather than more in-depth training on equipment operations.[42] This is particularly true for ATSS personnel coming from military backgrounds who already have relevant knowledge and skills. Staffing shortfalls that result in ATSS personnel not being able to take advantage of available training were also noted by ATSS personnel as impediments to professional development.[43]

---

40 ATSS personnel comment to committee during site visits to FAA facilities at Leesburg and Dulles, Virginia.

41 Austin Aurandt, acting manager, program management team, Air Traffic Control Facilities Directorate, AJW-2, FAA, presentation titled "Future Facilities" Program Overview to the Committee on Staffing Needs of Systems Specialists in Aviation, December 6, 2012.

42 Comments submitted to Staffing Needs of Systems Specialists in Aviation Stakeholder webpage, 2013.

43 Ibid.

OTHER CONSIDERATIONS FOR AN ATSS STAFFING MODEL

Performance Measures

An important consideration for any staffing model is the effect that inadequate staffing has on the goals of the organization. The ultimate measure of NAS performance is the availability of the equipment and facilities in good working order. One such related measure cited to the committee was "Adjusted Operational Availability," defined as the ratio of the total time the NAS was fully operational (i.e., not experiencing an outage) to the maximum time the NAS could have been fully operational over the time frame measured, such as an FY (FAA, 2011c). This measure gives an idea of how much of the systems and services were available to the NAS, but it subtracts out the planned nonavailability due to scheduled maintenance. In FY 2011, the FAA set an Adjusted Operational Availability target of 99.7 percent and achieved a level of 99.72 percent. The Adjusted Operational Availability measurement may present an overly optimistic picture of NAS maintenance. For example, because the NAS includes redundant systems, true outages of the NAS rarely occur. So an outage in one system within the NAS may be masked by another system providing the same functionality.

The FAA uses a myriad of internal measures and metrics to monitor performance as part of the NAS Performance Analysis System. Many of these metrics are well worth exploring in relation to modeling the resources required to maintain various NAS standards.[44] For example, there are intermediate measures of performance that provide an indication of whether there is understaffing or overstaffing, including scheduled maintenance backlog, staff overtime, and metrics that capture any temporary staff supplements from other work sites or temporary reallocation of personnel in the work site to other duties. Finally, the cost of a particular staffing level provides useful information for comparing alternatives and assessing levels of performance risk.

Risk Assessments

From the HSI perspective, risk influences every step of the system development cycle (from definition to end-of-life). Risk is an expression of potential loss; the loss may be loss of life, loss of equipment or property, loss of work days, loss of system or human functional capabilities, and/or other losses. Risk, in most staffing contexts, refers to the interaction between the probability of a negative event or hazard occurring and the severity of the consequences of the event or hazard. The expected value of the risk is summarized as the probability P multiplied by severity S. With ATSS staffing, risk may be related to the optimal staffing level: risk is lowered as staffing approaches optimal levels.

In a stochastic model[45] of staffing, risk can be estimated as the probability of adverse events and the time that systems are unavailable resulting from those events. In such a model, risk would be a direct function of staffing levels. Objective risk can be measured as a function of weighing factors that serve as contributing coefficients (such as fatigue, stress, training timelines, technological malfunctions, or maintenance demands) with variables that are part of the system (such as number of overtime hours an ATSS employee works, travel time to remote locations, or level of air traffic). Another way of assessing risk uses a combination of quantitative methods and qualitative methods that rely on judgments and decisions of experts. One common method to assess risk, which is represented in Figure 2-3 and

[44]See detailed listing of Outage, Availability, Restoration, and Reliability measures in FAA, 2011c.

[45]A stochastic model includes the inputs of time taken by ATSS personnel in all their tasks, but also incorporates the probabilities of unexpected events occurring that affect the time required to complete tasks such as equipment reliability, employee illness, and weather.

Hazard Classification

Hazard Likelihood Categories

FREQUENCY OF OCCURRENCE			Frequent	Likely	Occasional	Seldom	Unlikely
SEVERITY	Catastrophic	I	1E	1E	2H	2H	3M
	Critical	II	1E	2H	2H	3M	4L
	Marginal	III	2H	3M	3M	4L	4L
	Negligible	IV	3M	3L	4L	4:	4L

Hazard Risk Index

FIGURE 2-3 Hazard assessment matrix.
Abbreviations: Extremely high (E), High (H), Moderate (M), and Low (L), Hazard Risk Index Labels: 1 = Unacceptable, 2 = Undesirable with management waiver required, 3 = Acceptable with management review, 4 = Acceptable without review.
SOURCE: Swallom, Lindberg, and Smith-Jackson, 2003:505. Permission granted by John Wiley & Sons, Inc.

described by Swallom, Lindberg, and Smith-Jackson (2003), is based on a combination of graphical risk assessment tools provided by Kohn, Friend, and Winterberger (1996), Military Standard 882C (Department of Defense, 1993), and Roland and Moriarty (1990). The FAA employs a similar model construct (FAA, 2007a).

With this matrix, risk can be assessed in the ATSS staffing plan by conducting a facility visit followed by a what-if analysis of scenarios resulting from current or estimated staffing levels. For example, an event that would result in critical negative outcomes (e.g., severe injuries and/or large financial loss) and that would occur frequently in conditions of low staffing would be unacceptable and lead to extremely high risk. On the other hand, an event with similar outcomes that is highly unlikely to occur in low staffing conditions could yield an acceptably low level of risk. Thus, the table reflects both potential effects and likelihoods of risky events.

The 2006 report by the National Research Council on staffing for aviation safety inspectors suggested risk should be analyzed at two levels: (1) a detailed analysis focusing on aspects of "system design" (i.e., the confluence of factors that drive demand for ATSS); and (2) a macro-level analysis that focuses on "program risk management" (i.e., the approaches used to promote safety) (National Research Council, 2006). In the 2006 report, the committee considered risk an important factor in exploring the parameters of a staffing model and establishing staffing levels. Several aspects of the ATSS staffing situation increase risk. As indicated by stakeholders, risk is increased when hiring lags behind the need for qualified ATSS personnel. Lack of training or delays in training, both formal and informal, lead to understaffing, a workforce that has insufficient skills to perform the assigned work, or both. These consequences also increase risk. As previously mentioned, the demand for scheduled preventive maintenance and relatively unpredictable corrective maintenance add a level of risk that reflects a range of probabilities and uncertainty in the entire system. Geographic diversity of the NAS facilities also contributes to complexity and increases risk by limiting the number of certified ATSS personnel available.

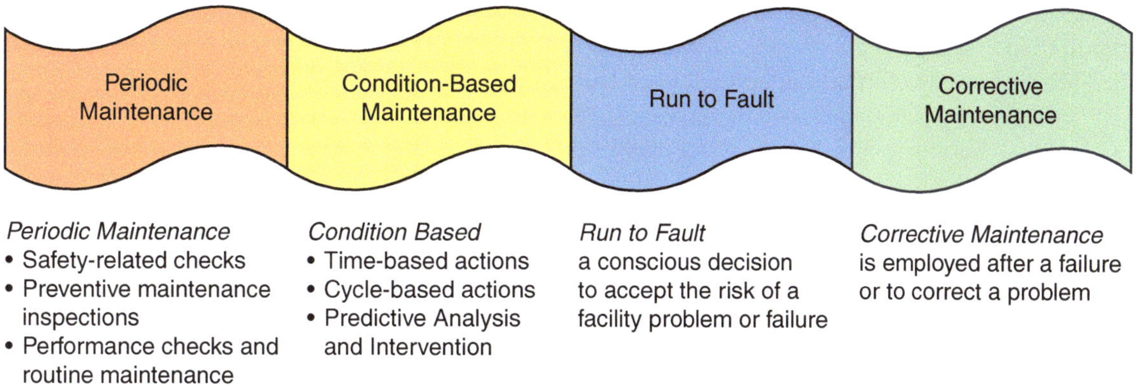

FIGURE 2-4 Reliability centered maintenance.
SOURCE: FAA, 2010.

Tracking Maintenance Activities

At present, the FAA has shifted ATSS work to a reliability centered maintenance[46] approach (FAA, 2007b, 2010) from a previous philosophy that stressed more frequent periodic maintenance and certification activity for many NAS systems. The implementation of an event-based certification process eliminates the requirement for periodic system and subsystem certification, but mandates certification prior to commissioning new equipment, upon requests following aircraft incidents, after any adjustment to the certification parameters, and prior to restoration after any modification or specified interruptions. Rather than more frequent scheduled maintenance activities on some systems, the philosophy of event-based certification has shifted to "run to fault," at which point the equipment would be inspected, repaired or restored, and certified to return to the NAS. Alternatively, failed equipment might also be decommissioned. Figure 2-4, taken from an FAA pamphlet titled *6000.15E Pocket Reference*,[47] shows a "shorthand" perspective of the evolved philosophy of reliability centered maintenance (FAA, 2010).

Remote Maintenance Monitoring (RMM) has been extensively implemented within the FAA (FAA, 2010). Bottino and Hughes (2004) assert that "reliability, suitability, and longevity of navigational aids, weather processors, and surveillance systems have improved due to the functionalities RMM systems provide." Although RMM systems continue to transform the ATSS environment, and NextGen systems are being implemented with significant reliability enhancements in mind, aging of the NAS legacy systems and the availability of critical parts for old equipment may counteract those advantages. Currently, ATSS personnel are required to update multiple nonlinked legacy systems, rather than a single, integrated system. Both advanced deployment of RMM and the utilization of modern, integrated Computerized Maintenance Management Software (CMMS) can help optimize utilization of all ATSS maintenance

---

[46]Reliability centered maintenance concepts were honed in the aviation realm and have since spread dramatically through other maintenance-related fields. Ideally, the whole state of reliability and maintainability best practices should be examined for careful application within the NAS, and lessons from the ATSS world should be shared with others. See Moubray (2001) for an excellent treatment of this subject.

[47]*6000.15E—General Maintenance Handbook for National Airspace System (NAS) Facilities Pocket Reference* (FAA, 2010) was superseded by *6000.15F* (FAA, 2011a). In the update, some guidance changes were made as Safety Risk Management specialists reviewed and concurred that the changes were categorized as having no safety impact and posed no risk to the NAS. It was finalized in the Safety Risk Management Decision Memorandum dated October 5, 2010.

resources. The FAA may incorporate elements of maintenance resources into an evolved CMMS architecture to help assess shift scheduling, inventory of spares, and optimal use of personnel to maintain the NAS. This new system should integrate at least the following:

- Facility, Services, and Equipment Profile data collected and stored in an electronic system to document the maintenance activities related to the NAS (Grant Thornton, 2011)
- The Remote Monitoring and Logging System used by Technical Operations to track the scheduled maintenance performed (Grant Thornton, 2011)
- Labor Distribution Reporting (LDR), which is used by Technical Operations to track the time spent on job tasks (Grant Thornton, 2011)

An evolved CMMS solution would help FAA resource planning and optimization of parts or staffing through the objective of moving closer to seamless systems that multiply productivity for the people. This contrasts with the current situation in which ATSS personnel feed similar information into multiple systems.

Balancing Budgetary Priorities

When ATSS staffing levels are adequate to perform prescribed maintenance activities, risk to NAS safety is minimized. At the same time, staffing levels will, in part, be determined by the cost of labor and other budgetary priorities. However, allowing staffing levels to be driven solely by cost is an unacceptable risk to the NAS. Thus, the interactions among staffing levels, NAS performance, and system costs require further exploration.

Staffing Model Considerations

Any staffing model requires data. LDR records were intended to provide accurate data on the time spent performing work at each facility, the specific job tasks undertaken, and the associated documentation of that work.[48] However, incorrect data resulting from either underreporting or nonreporting (which both management and labor agreed were generally due to the unwieldy structure of the LDR system)[49] result in unreliable inferences regarding the amount and type of work performed by ATSS employees. One example of the multiple problems with LDR is that time recorded for travel to a remote facility cannot be logged using the same code used for working at that facility. In addition, the administrative tasks that ATSS personnel must perform during every shift (e.g., time logging, maintenance logs) do not have LDR codes and are thus not recorded.[50] By comparison, the Simplified Automated Logging system likely provides a more accurate record of the time and types of work performed by ATSS personnel than does the LDR;[51] it could therefore contribute more useful data to a staffing model, once the data have been evaluated.

[48]Mike Perrone, president, PASS, AFL-CIO, presentation to the Committee on Staffing Needs of Systems Specialists in Aviation, December 6, 2012.

[49]Ibid.

[50]Comments submitted to Staffing Needs of Systems Specialists in Aviation Stakeholder webpage, 2013.

[51]Mike Perrone, president, PASS, AFL-CIO, presentation to the Committee on Staffing Needs of Systems Specialists in Aviation, December 6, 2012.

The committee investigation kept in mind an overall HSI approach across the nine major HSI domains, as they are essential elements in the success of the ATSS workforce in maintaining the NAS. For example, the size and cost of a workforce are dependent on the level of performance and safety deemed essential. As discussed in Chapter 1, the personnel, training, human factors, and manpower domains are interdependent. It should be noted that much of the committee's effort focused on the manpower domain. In this report the committee uses the terms *staffing models* and *staffing standards* to denote HSI manpower domain tools for the determination and management of manpower as a resource. Such tools support decisions about how many workers of what general types are needed to staff the organization and decisions on what the corresponding workload is.

The manpower requirement estimated by a model may be an overall aggregate number or the number of personnel by location or by work areas within each location. Depending upon the rigor and approach involved, the model could potentially account for skills, grades, and qualifications. The ATSS skill universe includes the five disciplines or skill areas described at the beginning of this chapter. Because of the current operations involving ATSS personnel and the requirements for appropriate certification, the supply and demand for each of these skill areas should be accounted for within the model.

Finding 2-2: A number of human resource issues, such as hiring procedures, training requirements, retirements, and military obligations, affect the number of qualified ATSS personnel who are available at any point in time to maintain the NAS.

Conclusion 2-2: The committee concludes that human resource issues such as retirements and succession planning considerations should be addressed in conjunction with any comprehensive manpower staffing model.

Implications for Staffing Models

Based on its understanding of the ATSS job and work environment, the committee noted several implications for a staffing model:

- It must capture the full extent of the NAS and its varied components, the geographic dispersion of facilities, and the staffing implications of travel time to equipment in remote areas.
- It must clearly identify domain disciplines in which ATSS personnel must be proficient to meet workload demand, and it must quantify the levels of expertise required.
- Performance measures or outcomes, both final (ultimate) and intermediate, should be included so that the model can provide predictions regarding the outcomes of a given staffing plan.

Recommendation 2-2: In accordance with the principles of human-systems integration, the FAA should build a robust staffing model that takes into account all of the following aspects of the ATSS job series, in addition to the time that ATSS personnel spend on preventive and corrective maintenance tasks:

- Training issues, time to schedule training, the time required to attend training, and the time of experienced ATSS personnel necessary to provide OJT
- Travel time to and from work sites
- Environmental challenges
- Time dedicated to military reserve service or family and medical leave
- Fatigue mitigation plans
- Safety factors
- LDR deficiencies and other data deficiencies

- Aging workforce and succession planning considerations
- FAA's Next Generation (NextGen) system
- Nontechnical task demands

SUMMARY

The job duties and work environment for ATSS personnel are extremely complex. The job series encompasses multiple disciplines and requires extensive training. Incumbents confront environmental and travel issues, are subject to the demands of shift work, and have demands on their time beyond their assigned technical responsibilities. The implementation of the NextGen system adds an additional layer of ambiguity and concern regarding ATSS workload. All of these issues are acknowledged by the stakeholders who provided input to the committee. Any staffing model for ATSS personnel that is intended to be accepted by appropriate stakeholders will need to address these concerns.

3

Considerations in Creating a Staffing Model

The primary challenge for the committee was to find ways to create effective staffing models to determine Airway Transportation Systems Specialists (ATSS) staffing level requirements in Technical Operations work sites and appropriately accommodate the various stakeholder concerns discussed in Chapter 2. To address this challenge, the committee reviewed the fundamentals of modeling in general as applied to developing staffing estimates, which is the subject of this chapter. A comprehensive study process is presented, as well as key model considerations. The chapter concludes with the quality factors against which a staffing model is evaluated. The review of these modeling fundamentals sets the stage for the evaluation of existing models and creation of recommendations for the use of modeling to successfully define and predict ATSS workforce requirements in future efforts.

WORKFORCE MODELING AS PART OF A LARGER CYCLE OF WORKFORCE PLANNING

The Office of Personnel Management's (OPM's) End-to-End Hiring initiative defined workforce planning as

> the systematic process for identifying and addressing the gaps between the workforce of today and the human capital needs of tomorrow. Workplace planning is based upon a set of workforce analyses which provide insight into how agencies can align their workforce to meet human capital goals and objectives that link to the agency's mission and strategic objectives. (Office of Personnel Management, 2008:12)

The workforce planning cycle as defined by OPM entails five basic steps as shown in Figure 3-1. Step two of this workforce planning cycle—analyze workforce, identify skill gaps, and conduct workforce analysis—includes much of the committee's task, which is to provide the Federal Aviation Administration (FAA) with guidance in determining the current ATSS workforce size and allocate ATSS personnel to match predicted workload. This portion of the cycle can be a difficult and poorly executed step of an overall workforce planning process, as developing tools to ascertain the kinds, numbers, and location of workers needed to accomplish an enterprise's goals and objectives can prove a tremendous

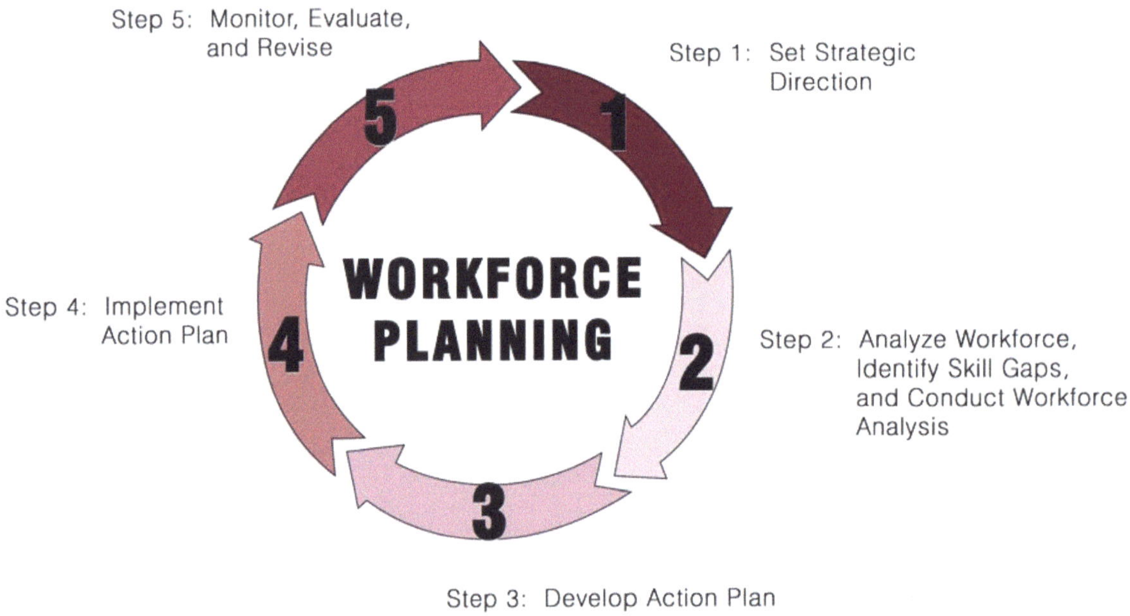

FIGURE 3-1 OPM's workforce planning cycle.
SOURCE: Office of Personnel Management, undated.

challenge. For a large enterprise, skipping the workload assessment/workload analysis dimensions and only performing a gap analysis on existing position structure and supply, then creating a plan to fill open positions, will likely be inadequate for defining the number of employees with particular skills sets and credentials needed in a variety of facilities and geographic locations.

Because ATSS personnel maintain tens of thousands of pieces of equipment of different types and at various stages of the equipment lifespan across a broad geographic area, and at a high level of operational readiness, defining and measuring the workload is formidable. Different philosophies about maintenance—for example, a philosophy of preventive inspections and maintenance versus one of "repair when the system breaks"—create a wide spectrum of potential staffing outcomes.[1] The expected levels of performance and tolerances for time between failures of systems may drive the need for extra shifts or ATSS personnel assigned to a particular problem, facility, or geographic location. ATSS technicians may be assigned to a particular task or may be in standby status on a shift and available via telephone for call-outs.

> All organizations base staffing decisions on a paradigm of the underlying production process [or the means by which work is accomplished], whether they do so explicitly or not. This conceptualization is often referred to as a staffing model. A staffing model is a formal representation of the mechanisms that drive the need for staffing resources. (National Research Council, 2006:4)

[1]As the FAA adopted reliability centered maintenance practices, some tradeoffs have already been carefully weighed and incorporated into the agency's guidance for technical operations.

Changes in the services provided and, in the case of Technical Operations, changes in the amount or type of equipment maintained should drive the types and numbers of ATSS personnel required. An effective staffing model should represent work done with existing processes, unless the processes modeled are deliberately modified to reflect anticipated changes in the work; significant change to existing processes require updating or refining the model to ensure its accuracy. If important factors that have an effect on staffing are identified and accurately measured, then the algorithms of a good model should provide useful standards or staffing projections.

VALUE OF PRACTICAL MODELS FOR ATSS PERSONNEL

In many public and private enterprises, human resources account for at least 50 percent of the cost of the operation and can consume a great deal more of the organization's financial resources.[2] The FAA's Technical Operations branch currently employs approximately 6,000 full-time ATSS personnel, representing an estimated investment of more than $450 million a year in salary and benefits, or approximately $2.25 billion over a 5-year budget cycle. The true fully burdened workforce cost (which includes 6,100 workers) is likely higher.[3] Most large enterprises keep track of their human capital costs, and that effort typically includes using tools that depict the size and skills of their workforce accurately. The output of well-designed modeling tools can strengthen the argument for a correctly sized workforce in budget discussions by providing clearer and reasoned estimates of the risks if the workforce has fewer people than the organization's missions demand. Although technology is essential to the FAA mission of keeping the national airspace safe for movement of passengers and freight, the right mix of talented human beings is also essential to achieve that mission.

There are many ways to acknowledge the value of the ATSS workforce. Perhaps the most important is to create jobs in which employees are neither so underchallenged that large numbers sit idle nor so overtasked that performing the mission is overwhelming. A properly sized workforce helps ensure achievement of the FAA's mission of maintaining the safety of the National Airspace System (NAS) at reasonable costs and levels of efficiency. Moreover, appropriate levels of staffing are likely to reduce turnover that is due to morale issues stemming from placing a responsibility on workers that cannot reasonably be met. An ancillary benefit to careful workforce planning is personal life balance for ATSS personnel.[4] In addition, the value of an accurate staffing model also has to take into account the value of a high functioning NAS that is both safe and efficient. Although these costs are generally recognized and can be estimated with varying degrees of precision, it would be impossible to calculate the exact cost of understaffing in terms of its impact on business and commerce. One outage may have far-reaching and costly impacts that are never fully identified. Despite the difficulty of specifying the exact dollar amount, a robust staffing model must consider the far-reaching effects of understaffing.

[2]For example, a 2011 report stated that 80 percent of U.S. Postal Service outlays were spent on labor costs (U.S. Postal Service, 2011). National Income and Product Accounts data from the Bureau of Economic Analysis indicate that approximately half of state and local government total expenditures are wage and benefit related (http://www.bea.gov/itable/index.cfm) [June 2013].

[3]This is an approximate and conservative estimate, given the previous negotiated floor/threshold of 6,100 workers. If 6,000 full-time workers were employed at a fully burdened cost of just $75,000 per year per worker (which is on the low side), the annual cost would be $450 million and the 5-year cost (assuming no inflation) would be $2.25 billion. The FAA employs more than 30,000 workers and for fiscal year (FY) 2013, the Technical Operations budget request was $1.7 billion, which included a request for authorization of 8,050 full-time equivalent (FTE) employees (Department of Transportation, 2012).

[4]Comments submitted to Staffing Needs of Systems Specialists in Aviation Stakeholder webpage, 2013.

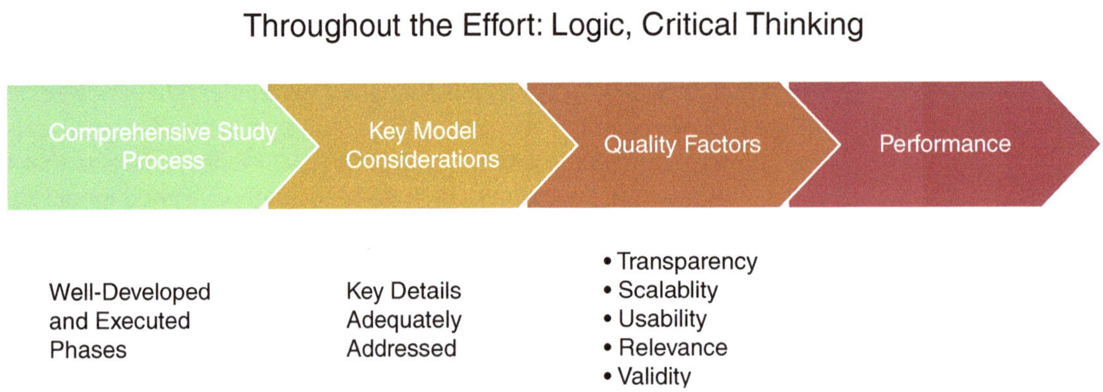

FIGURE 3-2 Steps for successful modeling.

CONCEPTUAL APPROACH TO MODELING USED BY THE COMMITTEE

The next section of this chapter presents the fundamental aspects of modeling that lead to success. Figure 3-2 highlights these components: (1) a comprehensive study process, (2) key model considerations, and (3) quality factors that can enhance the likelihood of (4) desired model performance. Because these components provided the basis for the committee's assessment of the current assumptions and methods used by the FAA to estimate ATSS staffing needs and for its recommendations regarding more appropriate approaches to staffing models, each component is described in more detail below. Experienced modelers rely more on logic than the rigid application of any given method for developing a staffing model (Law and Kelton, 2000).[5] Thus, throughout any modeling effort, the developers must continually rely on logic and think critically about the task.

Comprehensive Study Design Process

To be accurate in its estimates, a staffing model should be designed using a comprehensive development process that captures major drivers of ATSS workload at the appropriate level of detail and properly links the workload to the number of person-hours required to achieve the defined tasks of the job incumbents. Although it was not the intent of the committee to prescribe a detailed staffing model methodology, this report does discuss the steps in a generic logical model development process so that essential actions are considered and not overlooked in creating a specific model for ATSS personnel.[6]

[5]For a simulation approach, Law and Kelton (2000) provide examples of essential steps and considerations.

[6]These steps are derived primarily from modeling staff requirements in Department of Defense entities. The Navy Total Force Manpower Requirements Handbook, April 2000, lists five steps: Planning, Data Gathering, Data Analysis, Documentation and Reporting, and Implementation (U.S. Navy, 2000). The Air Force has used similar 6- and 7-step approaches. The Army once used a 12-step modeling algorithm but allows for many more variations today. The committee's point here is to focus not on the amount of steps used but on the employment of a logical, comprehensive, phased approach that includes certain deliberate activities to create viable manpower staffing models. A caveat is that the conditions under which the military services analyze staffing requirements are both similar to and decidedly different from those confronted by the FAA. These organizations all have ATSS-like positions whose incumbents are responsible for maintaining the equipment necessary to manage air traffic in the airspace. However, the work environment and work rules that may have an effect on staffing vary considerably. For example, the military services, unlike the FAA, all have a greater degree of control of their personnel. Furthermore, the FAA

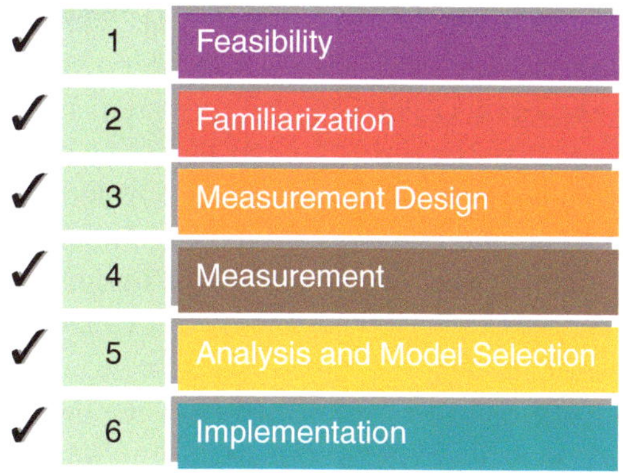

FIGURE 3-3 Logical design process: model development phases for comprehensive study.

The comprehensive modeling process described here consists of six phases: feasibility, familiarization, measurement design, measurement, analysis/model development and selection, and implementation. Most seasoned workforce modeling experts use a similar approach. For example, the Air Force uses its Management Engineering Program, which describes similar steps that have been refined over decades to produce generations of effective workforce staffing tools.[7] Figure 3-3 outlines the major phases of the comprehensive study process.

Phase 1. Feasibility

The objective of the feasibility phase is to determine if a modeling study effort should proceed or should be canceled or delayed due to problems such as nonstandardization, operational or organization instability, higher or conflicting priorities, and so on. The decision to continue development efforts is based on initial data- and fact-gathering concerning the responsibilities of job incumbents, the environment in which work is performed, and the resources available to the modeler such as time records, equipment lifespan data, etc. Two approaches to viewing work are commonly used: a work site approach and a work process approach. The work site approach focuses on a location and describes all the work that is done at that location. The work process approach focuses on a particular line of work and describes how it is performed in multiple locations. The environment to be studied includes dimensions such as the fiscal/budget situation, technological complexity of the work and equipment and anticipated changes, and the rate of change associated with the work performed. Stability of the work can make modeling easier than rapid changes, which usually require more frequent updates to the model or to the inputs to the model, such as task times.

---

must comply with work rules and contend with a labor union. Although these differences may not affect what steps need to be taken to develop a staffing model, they may affect how each step is implemented and what factors are taken into account.

[7]More information on the Air Force approaches can be found at AFI 38-201 and AFMAN 38-208 Volumes I and Volume II; Army Guidance includes Army Regulation 570-4 and publications from the U.S. Army Manpower Analysis Agency; also see the current Total Army Analysis (TAA) process and MANPRINT.

A critical question to ask is "Do stakeholders agree it is the right time to conduct a study?" A major consideration in answering it should be the level of effort, time, and resources required to complete a study in light of the outputs desired. If the decision is to proceed with the study effort, a study scope and framework are established to guide collection of information needed to plan and conduct model development. Stakeholders should take the time to carefully define and review study goals, scope, and milestones, as well as consider the potential limitations of the results.

A number of multi-level considerations are relevant to feasibility. Specifically, there appear to be a number of potential cross-level interactions among individual training and higher-order factors such as location and distance. The committee believes that the model would probably benefit from exploring such nonlinear and cross-level interactions.

A memorandum of agreement should be established between the modelers and the primary stakeholders that documents what the modelers plan to do, what time frame they will do it in, what will be required of various stakeholders and the organization, and what output should be expected. A study announcement should be developed and shared with appropriate stakeholders, who may include management representatives from various functions and locations, job incumbents, union representatives, and others, to inform them of the effort and their responsibilities and to engage their support.

Phase 2. Familiarization

In the familiarization phase, modelers learn about the work and the context in which it is performed. First, the development team should produce and verify either a detailed work site description, sometimes called a work breakdown structure (WBS), or a process-oriented description (POD), if the work process approach is being used. A WBS is usually created by taking major work categories or components and breaking them down into smaller and smaller subcomponents. A POD is designed to document functions by inputs, process, and outputs, and then identify the subcomponents or details of these process elements.[8] The WBS or POD should contain a fairly complete description of the various tasks performed in the work sites because it forms the basis for the staffing model. Creating a useful and accurate WBS or POD at the right level of detail is one of the most important outputs of this phase, as an accurate accounting of the activities that drive most of the worker effort is directly related to the accuracy and value of the staffing model output. It is also helpful to create a statement of conditions—that is, a description of the normal work environment and the operating challenges and unusual conditions faced by workers performing particular types of work in various locations.[9] Modelers also find it useful, if not essential, to capture an initial set of key baseline data, such as the present structure of the organization, the number of full-time equivalents (FTEs) funded and currently employed, the allocation of workers across the organization, and staffing information such as details about personnel accessions by location and specialty.

Another component of this familiarization phase is the identification of potential workload factors (i.e., those factors that affect the hours of available labor for a work site) and the data sources in which information about each factor reside. Historical data related to the number of employees, time to completion for various tasks, failures and outages, etc., can be useful for trend or regression analyses whose results can inform the model of staffing needs. If the organization does not maintain or does not usually collect data on some of these potential factors, it must consider how best to gather the information

[8]Unlike a classic WBS, the Air Force shift to a POD allows ready process mapping and modeling, and may tie more directly with specified outputs of the activities, which in turn may potentially be more directly linked with performance measures.

[9]It should be noted that U.S. Air Force manpower studies, and their classic end product, an Air Force Manpower Standard (AFMS) include a statement of conditions. For more information, see AF/A1MR (2011).

required for accurate modeling and continue to maintain the data bases related to these factors. Examination of documents related to the job under study, such as official guidance, directives, standards, policies, performance measures, and transformation plans related to the organization, the work, or the equipment can also increase the modeler's understanding of the job and of anticipated changes in the work.

Phase 3. Measurement Design

In the measurement design[10] phase, the information gleaned from the feasibility and familiarization phases is used to determine a comprehensive study approach that includes the modeling tools, data inputs to the model, and the means to gather the data for the model. A critical question for the study team is how the data relevant to the modeling task will be gathered. For example, the team might use interviews of subject matter experts, a time study based on samples of work, or a by-location, by-work-element shift profile analysis.[11] Any combination of methods for collecting data may be used, but the approaches to collecting data need to be clearly defined, preferably tested on a sample of the overall workforce, and then refined based upon the lessons learned in the test, prior to conducting full-scale data collection. In addition, the team must be aware of the potential impact on the people who provide the data of any intervention necessary for data collection, especially direct observations. Otherwise, the team may receive distorted information about the nature of ATSS work.

The measurement plan should define samples that are representative of the population and sufficient to make the types of statistical inferences necessary for modeling. When the job under study involves a large number of workers across many work locations, the modeler does not necessarily have to measure in detail the work of every person at every location; instead, a subset of workers and locations that represent adequately the overall population will be sufficient in most cases. The modeling effort needs to include enough data points to be representative of the various types of facilities, types of equipment and tasks, and work centers to be statistically significant. If the organization is investing in a model covering thousands of FTEs, a 90 percent confidence level or higher may be desired. At one extreme, a belief that 100 percent of a large population should be measured can incur excess costs and time that consume study resources. At the other extreme, only measuring a few locations or relying on a small input sample, in an effort to expedite the effort or save resources, is even more likely to produce an unrealistic model output—with disastrous results if applied to the whole workforce.

The quality of the job information gathered must be considered, and when data are deficient, steps must be taken to improve the accuracy of the information to be used in the model. Several approaches to data verification exist. For example, multiple data collection teams can gather data and measure work performance at different sites. If multiple teams are used to conduct measurement and data collection, the study team must provide guidance to standardize the methods for data harvesting. If instead a "same eyes" approach is used, one team travels to all locations to collect data. Some modelers use a workshop or series of workshops facilitated by the study leads to collect data from subject matter experts. Often, the best approach is a combination of methods for systematically studying the tasks required in the job, the frequency with which the tasks are performed, and the corresponding number of person-hours needed to accomplish the tasks properly.

---

[10]For more information, see U.S. Air Force (1995a, 2003).

[11]Time studies, work sampling, elemental time, and other methods are not discussed in depth here but may be researched more in *Introduction to Human Factors and Ergonomics for Engineers*, Lehto and Landry (2013), and other industrial engineering texts.

A measurement approach must be consistent with the later phases of analysis and model selection. Consequently, the study team must anticipate the types of models to be explored, designed, and ultimately implemented. At times, the phases of the study process are iterative, so that the modelers must reconsider earlier decisions based on decisions made in later phases. Often, the limitations of available data and the feasibility of collecting more robust data constrain the type of modeling possible; when accurate models are required, such constraints must be remedied with extensive data collection plans. However, costs are a relevant factor in most modeling projects, and the team, in conjunction with the organization's management, must decide what approaches to data collection are affordable. They must also consider the financial implications of understaffing and overstaffing if the model's validity is weakened by insufficient data collection.

Phase 4. Measurement

This phase involves the execution of the measurement plan created in phase 3 and refined through testing. Data collected in this phase contribute to model selection and serve as the input to the selected model. The quality of the data collected significantly affects the value of the model; thoughtful measurement can make or break the study. All data obtained in this phase must be consistent with the plans for the study and should be validated by examining the data for completeness, accuracy, and logical consistency.

Phase 5. Analysis and Model Selection

The purpose of model development is to depict accurately the worker to workload relationship in order to derive the number of workers required by function or discipline and by facility type. Often, correlation and regression techniques are employed to examine the data and determine the worker-workload relationship. Study experts frequently discover several subpopulations that should be grouped and then develop separate tools to portray the worker-workload relationships for each group. In the case of the ATSS modeling challenge, the five different types of facilities may be suitable for individual groupings. Alternatively, the five disciplines might form the basis for grouping. For example, a model for depicting Core/Large Airport requirements and a separate model for GNAS, or a model for Environmental and another for Communications, may produce more accurate results. Statistical tests of the relationship may be used to determine the sufficiency or best fit of the model equation.

The end result should be an equation with a related set of statistical tools that the organization can use to determine the staffing requirements. These tools are often used at the location level and then aggregated to obtain total system requirements. Ideally, algorithms produce a set of tables that indicate the correct number and skill mix for a work site to accomplish its mission sets. For example, the Air Force manpower management engineering process has built-in "Smart Sheets" that take workload factor data as input and produce electronic reports showing the number, skills, and grades of full-time workers required to match the workload.

The more transparent and accessible for use the model is to different levels of the organization, the more likely the model is to be embraced by personnel at those levels. However, access to the model output may be limited, based on the user's needs so as not to overwhelm the user with massive amounts of information that are not relevant to that user.

Model design should also take into account the model's adaptability to changing conditions. An effective model must accurately depict the current worker-workload relationships, but the better model also offers "scalability" so that the model can be easily updated as the work or the work environment change. For example, NextGen and the eventual removal of older equipment are expected to have an extensive effect on the work actually performed, as well as on the frequency with which many tasks are performed. Often a modular approach is used so that the relevant components of the model can be updated without overhauling the entire model. As with any other modeling effort, a sensitivity analysis would also be appropriate to assess how sensitive the model outputs are to changes in various input variables.

Another component of model design is adherence to good human-systems integration (HSI) practices, including safety and human factors concerns. The model and its output should ensure that the staffing levels reflect what is necessary to protect workers' health (U.S. Air Force, undated).

Often, the model design phase includes validation and verification[12] elements, especially for highly complex models. A rigorous verification process in which predictions are compared to real-world situations of the past for which outcomes are known is begun at the same time the model is being developed. Data from the validation and verification effort can be used to refine the model or enhance the data inputs to it.

The verification, validation, and acceptance (VV&A) processes used to improve the model and increase the organization's confidence in it can take other forms. For example, qualified operations research or staffing model experts, teamed together with functional experts, can evaluate the assumptions, data quality, and modeling algorithms and point out opportunities for improvement. VV&A activities should be practiced throughout the modeling effort, both before and after implementation.

Other, more robust, formal VV&A approaches may be useful and worthy of careful consideration; however, as Carson (2002) noted, "a model developer intermixes debugging, verification and validation tasks and exercises with model development in a complex and iterative process . . . it should also be noted that no model is ever 100% verified or validated." The final determinant of the value of the model will be the accuracy of the predictions regarding labor necessary to achieve the goals of the job class. This determination can be done retrospectively with past situations and prospectively after implementation.

Phase 6. Implementation

Implementation of a new staffing model can be complex and requires close attention to how the model is introduced. How the model is implemented will have an effect on the level of acceptance achieved throughout the organization. At some point, the recommended model must be presented to decision makers for approval for use. Revealing the "test" impact of the model to management and workers within a public-sector function with many diverse stakeholders can be challenging, as there will typically be perceived "gainers and losers" by location as the workforce is adjusted by the model results to match the work requirements. It will be useful to stakeholders to have an honest picture of the future staffing levels derived from the model, as well as an explanation of how they were derived.

Budgets also need to be adjusted before implementation, particularly when there are increases to the staffing levels. Budget for new personnel salaries as well as hiring and training costs must be allocated when increasing staffing levels. When staffing levels decrease, the costs of reductions in force and redeployments must be factored into budgets. The committee had several discussions regarding how an effective model would look and how it could predict an effective number of ATSS personnel necessary for maintaining the NAS in a safe, efficient, and effective manner. These discussions did not focus on a total number of ATSS personnel, but there was an understanding that, should the model generate a number greater than 6,100, the anticipated FAA budget would need to be quickly increased to avoid the

[12]Validation is the process of determining the degree to which a model or simulation and its associated data are an accurate representation of the real world from the perspective of the intended uses of the model. Verification is the process of determining that a model or simulation implementation and its associated data accurately represent the developer's conceptual description and specifications in DODI 5000.61 (Department of Defense, 2009).

negative implications for the safety and efficiency of the NAS. In that case, the FAA's Air Traffic Organization would have to employ risk mitigation to compensate for the less than sufficient staffing while the budget was approved and additional personnel were hired, trained, and assigned to the appropriate sites.

Conclusion 3-1: Dedicated budget requirements for the ATSS are likely to result from application of any comprehensive manpower staffing model and will need to be addressed.

Public announcements related to increases or decreases in head count must be crafted to help outsiders understand the situation and win the public's approval. Often, examples of locations where the work is radically different are persuasive in demonstrating how the local uniqueness was addressed. For example, higher levels of staffing in locations that experience special environmental conditions, such as corrosive salt water, extreme temperatures and weather, or extended travel to service remote equipment may serve to demonstrate the sensitivity of the model.[13]

Value of a Logical, Comprehensive Design Process

Following a comprehensive design process that contains the essence of the six phases described above should greatly enhance the likelihood of creating an effective staffing model that enables the workforce to achieve the organization's goals. Some of the phases overlap, and ideally, study leaders intentionally look backward and forward in the process so that the end result is logical, valid, and compliant with the stated purpose. In particular, data examination during the measurement and analysis phases may necessitate revised data collection procedures or additional research. Moreover, those who develop the model need to plan for future improvements to it as modeling methodology and data collection procedures evolve and as the FAA obtains greater understanding of the causes of variability in the tasks performed by ATSS. Insights gained at any phase can redirect the study in unexpected ways; thus, the study team needs to be not only flexible but also seasoned in handling unexpected situations and understanding which approaches are most likely to be effective in a given situation.

Recommendation 3-1: The FAA should execute a modeling process that allows for future improvements in data modeling techniques and applicability.

Key Model Considerations

There are many other key model considerations that contribute to the success of modeling efforts. In this section, the committee reviews important considerations that will enhance the staffing model.

Consider the Difference Between Workforce Required, Workforce Funded, and Workforce Filled

Staffing standards produced by a given model are not identical to authorized or filled positions; *required*, *funded*, and *filled* are three different ways to describe the workforce and the numbers required. Staffing models may generate a fairly useful recommendation for defining a *required* workforce that is often refined by highly knowledgeable staff and managers, who then must compete for necessary funding in a resource-constrained public sector environment. Thus, the *required* workforce is not the same as the

[13] These conditions are termed as a "variance," which is an adjustment to the model for FTE time added or subtracted from the core requirements and is used and described in Air Force manpower requirements determination literature such as Air Force Manual 38-208, Volumes 1 and 2 (U.S. Air Force, 1995a, 2003).

funded workforce. FAA headquarters can create policy and routines to apply standards on an ongoing, cyclical basis for the creation of staffing plans and projections, and can also provide authorization (i.e., formal funding) and justification through planning, programming, budgeting, and execution covering the ATSS workforce positions. Once positions are recognized and funded, they in turn must be *filled.* However, a filled workforce is not entirely dependent on hiring. Other tools of the human resource life cycle (recruiting, development, sustainment, retirement, and so on) affect the number of positions to be filled.[14] For example, a model could predict a requirement for 18 FTEs to perform communication systems maintenance in one location, while the budget process may only authorize funds for 16 in that area, and there may be only 14 persons actually "on board" as filled positions. However, a good staffing model will provide decision makers with information regarding the expected consequences of under- and over-staffing. If fewer positions than are needed are authorized, for example, the model may indicate that a maintenance backlog is likely to emerge or that the risk of nonavailability of the NAS may increase. If more positions are authorized than are currently in the job, the hiring-training-development cycle needs to begin. Table 3-1 provides an example of staffing in one location across the five skill sets and management.

TABLE 3-1 Notional Example: "Location X" Staffing for a Particular Point in Budget Year

ATSS Skills at Location X	Model Driven Requirement (REQUIRED)	Authorized or Approved Allocation (FUNDED)	Actual Fill (FACE)	Difference Between Filled Status and Authorized/Funded
Management	2	2	1	−1
Environmental	17	15	13	−2
Automation	19	18	17	−1
Communication	18	16	14	−2
Radar	21	18	21	3
Navigational Aid	7	4	5	1
TOTAL	84	73	71	−2

An advanced modeling system for a large enterprise may have both short term (1-2 years) and longer term (out to approximately 5 years) staffing requirements. The difference between the two estimates provides forewarning to the organization that changes in staffing levels are likely to occur. Proactive organizations build staffing-process ramps to increase or decrease the number of individuals with the skills to match the current staffing needs that are determined by changing equipment, services, and budget realities. Once the organization determines the extent of change that is likely to occur, it must adapt other systems (recruiting, hiring, training, etc.) and acquire the necessary funding.[15]

[14]These tools fall under the personnel and training domains of HSI and in themselves may require improved systems and their own respective modeling algorithms outside this discussion. Examples are maintenance training throughput calculations and attrition/retirement/hiring estimating tools, among others.

[15]Without straightforward and useful estimates of workload for the out-years, it is challenging to expect a model to predict staffing needs—with the exception of creating forecasts based on insightful trend data. Air Force manpower data systems usually show positions for multiple quarters/years out in the budget cycle, and future adjustments are often calculated based on known changes in quantity and type of weapon systems that will be present or approved as missions change.

Consider the Difference Between an Allocation and a Sufficiency Model

The National Research Council conducted a study for FAA aviation safety inspectors in 2006 that had a charge similar to that of the current study on ATSS staffing. Many of the former committee's considerations at that time are applicable to the current task. Therefore, the present committee has quoted liberally from that prior report in this section. The following passage, for example, is directly applicable to the current study, with a few word changes to apply it to ATSS staffing:

> [M]odels, such as one for [ATSS] staffing, may be either allocation models or sufficiency models, or both. An allocation model is one aimed at distributing available resources equitably and effectively irrespective of their collective adequacy, whereas a sufficiency model is designed to predict the resources needed to sustain system performance at what is deemed an acceptable level. A sufficiency model is more difficult to develop. It requires the organization to make decisions about, and set standards for, acceptable performance and to develop performance measures so that outcomes can be evaluated against those standards (i.e., it can be empirically validated).
>
> [B]y providing an estimate of the resources necessary to meet policy and safety goals, a sufficiency model can be the most rigorous way to determine staffing needs and to support budget requests for [ATSS] positions.
>
> [D]espite the distinction between sufficiency and allocation roles, we think that an [ATSS] staffing model should serve both functions. That is, it should be able to estimate aggregate staffing demand, provide predictions regarding the consequences of alternative levels of staffing, and help guide the allocation of resources across functions, regions, and offices. (National Research Council, 2006:32, 39, 40)

Consider the Essential Features of the Situation to Be Modeled

"[T]he more faithfully a model captures the essential features of its real-world counterpart, the better able it may be to fulfill its intended function" (National Research Council, 2006:30). A powerful example used elsewhere in government, by the U.S. Air Force, is the model employed to understand, predict, budget, and allocate aircraft maintenance manpower. Mathematical representations of aircraft maintenance processes, repair networks, and component failure rates allow analysts to study enormous amounts of data and apply that data to predict with reasonable accuracy, for example, the number of Air Force maintenance personnel required to service and support a wing of fighter aircraft in order to provide a specified desired sortie generation rate. This predictive power is bounded, of course, by access to the necessary data and by changes within the system that require updating within the model. Models typically represent the relationship of variables through algorithms and equations that may vary in complexity and formalization.[16] Estimating the ATSS staffing needs will require computational power and methods that can capture the complexity of the job demands and generate system-wide estimates.

Consider Whether the Model Should Be Descriptive or Predictive

The 2006 report on Aviation Safety Inspector staffing contains a good explanation of whether a model should be descriptive or predictive. That account is quoted here with additional wording for clarification and application to ATSS staffing:

[16]For example, the relationship to demand for meals served and the staffing of a food service operation may be modeled simply as a straight line approximation of a factor of additional workers per incremental change in how many meals are required per day.

> [M]odels are generally characterized as either descriptive or predictive. Descriptive models typically document the structure and processes of a system, but they do not add a computational component to enable predictions about system behavior as a function of system design. An information flow diagram for a business process is an example of a simple descriptive model. [It shows] the steps, decisions, and outputs of a process, but alone does not offer insight in terms of the capacity or throughput of the system. Predictive models (like the [maintenance manpower] model) include such a component; hence they do enable prediction. In this project we have focused on predictive models because our charge is to articulate methods for determining the appropriate numbers and types of [Airway Transportation Systems Specialists] as a function of the factors that drive the demand for their services. Unless a staffing model can predict with some level of precision how well the [maintenance and service providing] system will perform given the need structure, it would be impossible to estimate appropriate staffing levels [objectively]. (National Research Council, 2006:30)

Consider Whether the Model Should Contain Stochastic or Deterministic Elements

Models can also be stochastic or deterministic.[17] The 2006 report includes an in-depth treatment of this subject.

> Stochastic models, a prominent form of which is the Monte Carlo simulation model, attempt to take into account the unpredictable elements of system behavior, whereas deterministic ones do not. For example, [the repair frequencies and time required for each repair of various national airspace subsystems] cannot be predicted with 100 percent accuracy even under optimal circumstances because of unknown factors. (National Research Council, 2006:30-31)

> Almost every system has some elements of uncertainty in it, so the question is not whether variability exists but rather how important it is to the system behavior that the model is designed to predict. If ignoring the variable nature of the system is likely to lead to inaccurate predictions or, equally important, a failure to recognize potential staffing risks, then stochastic modeling techniques should be [considered]. However, if the variability is not likely to [significantly] affect model predictions, or the variability is small and unimportant, a deterministic model—one that [minimizes treatment of] the stochastic properties of the system—should suffice. (National Research Council, 2006:31)

These unpredictable elements include an array of factors such as the reliability of individual components within each device, employee illness, weather, corrosion, and ease of access affecting the time required to complete tasks. Equipment failures are inherently stochastic. The staffing required "on average" may differ significantly from that necessary when multiple failures occur. A stochastic model provides insights on the risks associated with low probability events that may have significant consequences and potentially high costs.

A deterministic approach to modeling will typically produce the same results for FTEs needed when the same coefficients or work counts are used, because probability or variation is either not addressed or removed intentionally through the use of averaged process times. A deterministic approach may involve many input variables, but in simple terms can be represented as an equation where the FTE requirement y is a function of multiple inputs $x_1, x_2, \ldots, x_n$. A potential risk of deterministic models is that they predict staffing demand based upon mean values (i.e., average conditions), rather than recognizing that staffing demand per shift may be significantly greater (or less) than average values due to stochastic factors such as multiple failures.

[17]A deterministic model is a function of multiple inputs such as the type of equipment and the nature of the task to be performed. Law and Kelton (2000) provides fundamentals on how to go about addressing many stochastic situations and incorporating them into practical model designs.

The committee that wrote the 2006 staffing report noted that a deterministic model can provide sufficient predictive power to yield "fairly straightforward answers to a number of key staffing questions." While the complexity and cost of a stochastic model can be high, it is important to incorporate some stochastic elements that more accurately reflect reality. "It is important to recognize that both the stochastic model and the deterministic model can produce useful expected values for an outcome" (National Research Council, 2006:31, footnote). Thus, to address the immediate concerns of ATSS staffing, the creation of an initial series of deterministic algorithms should be followed by development of robust simulations and queuing models to fully assess stochastic elements of the ATSS job.

Stochastic models provide a better notion of the potential staffing risk associated with unusual events, such as multiple failures. In the ATSS staffing situation, stochastic modeling may incorporate, for example, the probability that the appropriate number of ATSS specialists will be available to meet the demands of required maintenance, because it will take into account queuing issues (e.g., surges and unscheduled multiple maintenance demands) and the stochastic nature of factors driving the need for services or repairs.[18] Hecht and Handal previously developed and demonstrated a prototype model they called SMART 4, which explored relationships between maintenance staffing, mean time between outages, mean time to restore, facilities, and other key ratios (Hecht and Handal, 2001; Hecht et al., 1998, 2000). Hecht and Handal's pioneering work may be a good starting point for bridging from standard deterministic models (such as ratio unit time equations per equipment or service and evolving support) and stand-alone powerful modeling and simulation tools for NAS resource allocation analysis. They also noted that these powerful simulation tools have been possible to create for some time, but their practical application has been bounded by the cost and complexity of implementation (Hecht et al., 2000). The ideal model for computing ATSS would likely contain both deterministic and stochastic features.

Consider the Critical Data Required for Analysis or That Drive Workforce Demand

The 2006 report on aviation safety inspector staffing explained the data required for analysis or for driving workforce demand; that explanation is reproduced here with added wording where applicable:

> [T]he distinction between the underlying predictive model and the *data* needed to make predictions using the model is critical. A model is created on the basis of the inherent properties of the system that drive its behavior. In the case of the aviation safety inspection system [maintaining the integrity of the NAS systems and services,] this includes factors that drive demand for [ATSS] resources and how these [ATSS] resources are deployed in response to that demand. However, even if these relationships are understood and well represented in a quantitative model, the model is worthless without the data that enable meaningful and realistic predictions. (National Research Council, 2006:32)

Modeling the relationship between staffing levels and the number and type of equipment maintenance needs in the NAS by region requires collecting data by region. Without a reliable baseline count and ongoing accounting or data systems that contain this information, there is no practical way to create such a model. Because modeling and data collection are interdependent, the cost of developing and sustaining data collection systems to feed into modeling must be considered. This is not to say that only "easy to collect" data should be used in the model. Key data that have not been readily available in the past should not be ignored, and methods to gather these data in a straightforward, economical manner should be developed. Too often, analysts have created an interesting but impractical manpower determination tool because of difficulty in routinely gathering the data required for the model's input

[18]For a primer on stochastic modeling and simulation concepts relevant to the ATSS maintenance environment, see Beichelt and Tittman (2012:Section III).

variables. As noted above, a critical step in the model development process is determining the source of input data and verifying its reliability.

Consider Task Duration and Data Validity Issues[19]

The utility of a model depends on the data used to populate the model as well as the structure of the model itself. Validity is defined as the extent to which a measure represents the construct being measured. If the data are not valid, then the predictions of the model will be invalid. For example, a valid measure of the time that Task X will take for completion, will be one that is accurate. If task duration estimates are based on workers who have not fully learned the task or conditions that do not represent the normal environment in which the task is performed, then the time estimates will not be valid measures of the time for completion under usual conditions. However, such measures may be valid measures of the time to complete a task under those unusual conditions.

Another confounding factor in making accurate estimates in task time completion is the bias in human judgments. Unless time estimations are made by a third party, the judgments may be consciously or unconsciously skewed. For example, a tedious task may be perceived by a subject matter expert to have taken longer than it actually did. Alternatively, a subject matter expert who likes to take his/her time in completing certain types of tasks may indicate a longer time than necessary to ensure the work can be completed at the preferred pace.

The validity of a measure is limited by its reliability, that is, the extent to which a measure is free from error and repeated measurements of the same entity (e.g., the same task, event, or object) yield similar values. If the reliability is low, then so is the validity. If the duration of task i is highly variable, a measure of duration based on the mean will have a large standard deviation. While the measure may be reliable, it may not be an accurate estimate of task duration in all situations. The actual time for task i could be almost constant, but the measurement process (such as relying on subject matter experts' estimates) may be error-prone and thus unreliable. Measurement reliability can be improved by using better methods of data collection; the inherent variability of the task itself is best dealt with by using stochastic models rather than deterministic models.

The other issue in collecting and using duration data is that of granularity. For example, the duration of an off-site maintenance task will be composed of at least two components: travel time and core task completion time. These two components will be affected by different variables, that is, travel distance, terrain, weather, and traffic for travel time; task complexity and ATSS personnel competence level for core task time. If the two subtasks are separated, simpler models can be built for each. Times for completion of the component tasks can be added to obtain the total time for the off-site task. This task decomposition can be taken to lower and lower levels, eventually ending at the element level of predetermined motion-time systems. Synthetic time estimates for new tasks can be computed by aggregating the known times for each element in the task.

There are three means of collecting data on task duration, each with different levels of reliability, validity, usefulness, and simplicity of use.

1. Subject Matter Expert Estimates. Asking supervisors or incumbents to estimate durations of tasks that they have performed in the past is simple and low-cost but generally quite unreliable. Human memory and judgment suffer from well-known biases (Kahneman et al., 1982) that potentially affect

[19]For more information, see Kahneman et al. (1982) and Bisantz and Drury (2004).

both reliability and validity of such estimates. Emerging technologies such as mobile devices and other electronic tracking devices may provide ways of obtaining more accurate time estimates in the future.

2. Historical Data. There are existing data bases such as the Remote Monitoring and Logging System and the Labor Distribution Reporting system that capture actual times for task completion contemporaneously and appear to have some relevance for estimating task durations. The data in these data bases were collected for different purposes (Bisantz and Drury, 2004), and so applying them to duration estimation for staffing models may not be reliable. Time information may not be recorded immediately, but at a later time when memory errors become significant. Typically such data bases only record total task duration rather than more meaningful and useful components as noted above. To improve the confidence in historical data or in subject matter experts' judgments, their accuracy may be verified by performing checks such as stopwatch measurement of task duration on a sample of the data.

3. Direct Time Study. A third approach is to observe directly the performance of the task and its components and record their durations. Time studies are an expensive proposition if a large amount of data is required, but the results generally have high reliability and validity. Best practices for conducting such time studies cover factors such as how many tasks to time, what degree of component decomposition to use, and how to select tasks and operators for observation and timing. If tasks change appreciably from time to time and situation to situation, then overall task durations will also change, requiring additional data collection and associated expense. If task components are measured and only a few components of the task change, costs can be reduced by only remeasuring that portion of the task that has changed.

Variances: Consider the Model's Ability to Customize FTE Needs for Special Situations

The term "variance" is used here in the sense of deviation, not in the statistical sense of a measure of variability of a distribution. Variances adjust core requirements either by increasing (positive variance) or decreasing (negative variance) earned FTE increments at specified location(s) or situations due to unique mission or environmental differences. Many models are often created to predict the average FTE requirement per various levels of workload demanded. Such models thus seek to capture the manpower required to do work that is common to all applicable locations. However, in actual work settings, certain processes or work activities are frequently not performed at all locations. Moreover, operational conditions at a location are not always the "average" conditions depicted within the model. If relevant and significant, these conditions can be addressed through calculation of positive or negative variances for the given location and situation.

For instance, a mission variance can add or subtract hours for location-specific required work that is not addressed in the work site description (a positive variance) or work identified in the work site descriptions but not performed (a negative variance). These differences in work should be documented, evaluated, and approved at appropriate level(s) as a matter of policy, not just through a local team leader's preference.

An environmental variance adjusts hours for required tasks that are addressed in a work site description but are affected by environmental differences among locations (i.e., mountainous territory or snow). The need for environmental variances in NAS maintenance may be based on challenges related to snow removal, need for de-icing of equipment, effects of a marine/salty environment on required corrosion control activities, effects of geographical separation on travel times, presence of remote versus on-site equipment or service monitoring capability, etc. For example, Technical Operations locations that maintain "inside the fence" systems may earn a normalized FTE requirement for the equipment maintenance tasks, while locations that maintain similar equipment at remote sites may receive a positive environment variance. In such circumstances, a "calculator" may be built into the model to compute the variance for travel time based upon number of times the team must go to the remote site.

It is usually not cost-effective to pursue and document variances that drive small adjustments. When building staffing models for small organizations, a half-FTE change may be worth documenting; however, for large organizations, the study team may establish a larger FTE value threshold for including variances in the model.

Consider Various Components of Total Staff Time

Ideally, any advanced modeling effort needs to address various components of total staff time, including direct productive time, indirect productive time, nonallowed time, nonavailable time, and on-call time and other work situations (U.S. Air Force, 1995a:53-58).

Productive time is time workers spend doing work that is essential to achieve their mission. There are two categories of productive work activities: direct work and indirect work. Direct work activities are required by guidance, technical orders, or directives; are essential to and directly support the work site's mission; and can be identified with a particular service or end product. Direct work activities are considered productive work that must be accomplished as part of the organization's primary mission. The time required for direct work tasks should be documented by task, whereas indirect work may be quantified either through similar means or by applying a previously computed and agreed upon indirect allowance factor to the total direct hours.[20]

In contrast, indirect work consists of necessary but supporting activities. Indirect work is performed in support of the function, does not add value to a particular end product, and may not be readily identifiable with a specific output or service. Common examples of indirect work include participating in human resource activities, giving management direction, preparing reports for higher level review, attending meetings, and housekeeping activities. If indirect work is not measured independently, then the analysts need to create an allowance factor and apply that factor as part of the model algorithm by crediting the measured hours of direct work with a percentage increase based on the indirect allowance factor.

The design of measures of critical data such as time to complete tasks and the careful collection of that must neither omit measurement of some kinds of data nor double count them. In particular, work dimensions such as travel, training, and supervisory tasks need to be carefully and consistently accounted for to ensure inclusion without double or triple counting. For example, if the enterprise-wide mean travel time associated with preventive maintenance of a specific type of navigational aid were credited to the task "maintains navigational aid type X" and included in the total average direct process time, then travel for such activities should not be re-counted as a separate indirect activity. As discussed above, substantial location-specific deviations from the mean travel time could potentially be computed as a positive or negative environmental variance. Similarly, the model should not credit travel at each subcomponent of the task "maintains navigational aid type X" because the travel occurred only one time. Nor should travel be counted for all tasks performed when a worker made only one trip but performed preventive maintenance checks on all of the equipment at the remote location.

---

[20]U.S. Air Force requirements determination analysts sometimes choose not to perform indirect task measurement for every function, as the Air Force has created separate standard indirect allowance task descriptions and factors (U.S. Air Force, 2011).

Nonavailable time is time that is directed and approved by management. During this time, the worker is not available to perform direct or indirect productive tasks. Examples of nonavailable time include approved leave, medical appointments, additional, directed duties such as serving as a voting liaison or office security officer, and time spent in approved education and training. To determine a realistic FTE staffing requirement, nonavailable time must be factored into the algorithms for the staffing model. When accounting for nonmandatory leaves such as annual leave or medical leave in a staffing model, the actual documented use of leave and not the maximum days allowed should be used; otherwise, the model results may be artificially inflated.

Allowances for days off, holidays, leave, and medical absences need to be decided on and approved (U.S. Air Force, 1995a). The original FAA modeling efforts dating from the 1980s and 1990s took many of these into account, and Order 1380.40C documents the treatment of the different dimensions (FAA, 1992). Categories of allowable time, such as Labor Distribution Reporting (006), Watch Schedules (031), Working Hours (032-036), Holidays (038), Annual Leave (040), Sick Leave (041), Family and Medical Leave (043), Leave for Special Circumstances (044-045), and other such factors are specifically defined in the current labor agreement between the Professional Aviation Safety Specialists (PASS) and the FAA, signed on December 16, 2012 (Professional Aviation Safety Specialists, 2012). Other considerations such as allowed time for meals, breaks, and rest should be considered and carefully defined. It should be noted that some of the variances in allowances will be stochastic.

Personal, fatigue, and delay (PFD) factors may be incorporated into a staffing model to account for necessary breaks, trips to the restroom, or other realistic and valid activities.[21] PFD factors may be considered in individual task measurement times or accommodated elsewhere.

On-call Time and Other Work Situations. On-call time is a period of time when an off-duty worker is available for work at a specified off-duty location and can be reached by telephone or other means. When authorized work is required and cannot be deferred to the next shift or work day, a work measurement effort should credit the work site with productive time expended and the travel time needed to get to the job site and return to the off-duty location. Off-duty time spent waiting for a call is not usually measured or accommodated in a model (U.S. Air Force, 1995a). However, because the FAA agreement with PASS regarding ATSS personnel contains a provision for Compensated Telephone Availability, such time should be considered in the model design process to optimize shift schedule requirements for meeting peak outages or demands (Professional Aviation Safety Specialists, 2012).

Often, the term "standby time" is used to explain the time a worker is awaiting work. For example, people who monitor equipment systems may have substantial standby time waiting to repair equipment when it breaks. A study team can measure and include standby time in a model when such duty is required and no other productive work (direct or indirect) can be accomplished. Workers who are loaned to perform another function's tasks should generally not be accounted for or included in a model for their own function.

[21]For more information, see Lehto and Landry (2013).

Consider Incorporating Shift Profile Analysis into the Model Development Approach and Model Application Tools

Maintaining equipment and providing services for a robust and safe NAS can require ATSS workers to be at work, available, or on call for long periods of a day. Coverage of the NAS components 24 hours a day, 7 days a week is not uncommon in many locations. Normal work hours in a traditional week schedule are 8.5 hours per day, including a meal break, for 5 days each week, with exceptions for alternate work schedules such as 10 hours per day for 4 days a week, or for overtime and Compensated Telephone Availability. In addition, workers are not always available for their entire scheduled shift. Activities such as annual leave, sick leave, military leave, training, and travel to remote sites all result in compensated workers who are not available to perform the tasks assigned to them during their shift.

A careful analysis of the shift scheduling and the work performed during shift can help optimize the total system workforce requirements for an organization. For example, the Air Force uses shift profile analysis to determine the amount of time its maintenance workers are available for direct work.

Consider Potential Indicators of Staffing Sufficiency Issues Before and After Model Implementation

Seasoned work analysts often check three indicators of staffing sufficiency: (1) use of overtime, (2) level of work site backlog, and (3) use of shortcuts to accomplish work. Examination of data in each of these areas can help to reveal the extent of understaffing or overstaffing.

Use of Overtime. Overtime can be useful for addressing greater needs for personnel due to peak work demands or temporary loss of personnel. However, excess use of overtime (or of borrowed workers from other organizations and contract workers) may indicate that the threshold staffing levels or shift schedule designs are not optimal within a work site. Steady use of large amounts of overtime can signal shortfalls in available "regular shift" FTEs, either from inaccurate staff targets, poor allocation, or inadequate fill action. In addition, high overtime utilization may indicate less than ideal management practices, which may lead to fatigue or vigilance problems not conducive to high levels of job performance nor ultimately to effective maintenance of the safety of the NAS.[22]

Work Backlogs. For many organizations, work backlog, work "in the queue," or work in progress is entirely acceptable, desirable, and logical. For the ATSS enterprise, it appears logical that periodic maintenance inspections and preventive maintenance activities would be pending for some period of time, but not necessarily postponed for an extended time. Presumably, the longer the period of time these activities are deferred beyond some limit, the higher the inherent risk to the NAS. Some work associated with almost any activity can be deferred, but work deferred indefinitely can be a sign of insufficient resources to meet the work demands. An important question for modelers to explore is whether or not the backlogs are reasonable and growing or decreasing over time, and why (Ouvreloeil, 2001).

Backlogs of work are not always attributable to staffing deficits. Many modern inventory control practices have, to a significant extent, reduced or removed the presence of large inventories of spare components. Some maintenance delays may be attributed to the unavailability of parts, not the unavailability of skilled ATSS workers to perform the work. The Air Force, for example, tracks metrics associated with the nonavailability of parts in order to analyze and improve logistics for aircraft maintenance processes (U.S. Air Force, 2009).

[22]For more information on overtime considerations, see Capshaw (2011).

Use of Shortcuts. The FAA operates within a formal Safety Management System that has available an array of tools and resources to prevent, identify, and analyze risk, including risk management through maintenance policy and procedure changes (FAA, 2007a). Nevertheless, on-scene work measurement or expert workshop review of tasks and times for many other maintenance-related fields have shown that a work site may occasionally employ shortcuts or deviations from standard practices that are not permitted or described in technical guidance in order to provide a service or maintain the required systems. Employing these shortcuts could be a valid innovation if properly studied and approved, but may unfortunately create a hidden level of risk within the system and long-term negative effects overall. In the modeling arena, if the time required for procedures officially documented in the Technical Operations guidance is accurately measured, but in practice the work site operates differently from the guidance for whatever reasons, the time estimates are likely to be inaccurate. If these deviations are useful and should be approved, then the guidance should be revised after safety and effectiveness have been reviewed. The underlying rationale for the use of shortcuts may, however, relate to perceptions of time pressure, poor training, or a lack of updated guidance. Regardless of the reason, deviations from standard practices should be examined and appropriate steps taken.

Quality Factors

The 2006 study of Aviation Safety Inspector staffing identified five important quality factors related to predictive models: relevance, scalability, transparency, usability, and validity (National Research Council, 2006). Box 3-1 defines these five factors, which were used by the current committee as criteria when reviewing the FAA's current and planned modeling efforts for ATSS personnel.

The 2006 report emphasized the importance of validity in assessing the value of a model:

> Validity is the final and, in many respects, the most critical feature. The extent to which the predictions of the model correspond to the actual, real-world outcomes constitutes its validity. Indeed, the most powerful means of evaluating a model's worth—the ultimate proof of the pudding—is the direct comparison of predicted with observed outcome (criterion) measures when such measures are obtainable. It is often the case that the ultimate criterion (i.e., [NAS] safety) is not directly measurable in any practical sense, so the model's predictive validity must be estimated against surrogate criterion measures. (National Research Council, 2006:33)

The prediction of outcomes associated with alternative levels of staffing is a necessary condition for the model to be testable and its validity assessed. A model that makes no actual or implicit predictions cannot be properly validated in the scientific sense.

> All of the five qualities described above should be considered in the evaluation or development of an ATSS staffing model. They apply equally to models that the FAA has used or is using as well as to any future modeling effort it may undertake. (National Research Council, 2006:34)

SUMMARY AND CRITERIA FOR ASSESSING MODELING

A starting point for developing or assessing a staffing model is to review the nature of the work, the environment under which the work is conducted, and the manner in which the work is accomplished. The committee's assessment of the work and the environment suggested that a viable staffing model for ATSS should

BOX 3-1
Quality Factors

Relevance—capture right level of detail. Relevance concerns the extent to which the model addresses the important portions of the issues for which it is designed and, equally important, the extent to which it excludes extraneous or marginally relevant issues or data. Does the model capture all of the important ATSS workload drivers? Does it operate at the right level of detail?

Scalability—usefulness for aggregation at higher levels, or predicting ATSS staffing needs by type of organization/facility, division or geographical region, or by required skill or discipline?

Transparency—ease of understanding, or the extent to which the model can be explained and understood by users of the model and those affected by decisions based on model implementation.

Usability—ease with which the model can be implemented and enhanced to make the predictions for which it was designed. Does it have an interface that is sufficiently intuitive to enable the model users to enter data efficiently and accurately? Is it appropriate to the skills and preferences of the intended users? Are the results presented in ways that support decision making? Can the model easily be updated to reflect changes in the ATSS work requirements and environment or changes in FAA policy?

Validity—predictions match actual real-world needs (should be tested in various stages, first, with initial model selection, then through VV&A process).

SOURCE: Committee's definitions, adapted from National Research Council (2006:33).

- capture the full extent of the NAS, the geographic diversity across facilities, and the staffing implications of travel time for equipment in remote areas;
- clearly distinguish and quantify domain disciplines required in achieving workload demand; and
- include performance measures or outcomes, both final (ultimate) and intermediate, in order to provide predictions regarding the outcomes of a given staffing plan.

A staffing model for ATSS should be "sufficient" in that it estimates staffing necessary to accomplish a given workload and is not simply a model that allocates a predetermined level of staffing across work sites. Moreover, because the nature of the workload itself—repairing equipment that fails—has an inherent stochastic component, serious consideration should be given to developing a stochastic staffing model. Furthermore, the model should be able to predict consequences associated with staffing at various levels, and these predicted outcomes should closely relate to what is actually observed at actual staffing levels. Chapter 3 has discussed the potential criteria for model evaluation. Chapter 4 will review the past and present FAA models used for the ATSS workers and examine how these models compare to some of the modeling philosophies that this chapter has explained. It also provides further recommendations that incorporate considerations introduced in this chapter.

Drawing on the previous discussion of the ingredients for successful modeling (i.e., a logical design process, key model considerations, and vigilance in seeking to attain the five quality factors), the committee created a checklist or set of criteria, shown in Box 3-2, with which to evaluate past models, models in progress, and other potential modeling approaches for the ATSS workforce. This checklist is intended as an aid to a modeler considering the criteria to use when designing a model for ATSS employees of the FAA.

BOX 3-2
Potential Criteria for Model Evaluation

Area 1. Logical Design Process

- Comprehensive Design
  - Measurement Design—comprehensive plan with steps documenting study approaches, objectives, means to gather and interpret the data, well-considered sample sizes and sites, amount of information to be harvested, with testing and refinement elements included
  - Data Type/Sources—logging and tracking of data such as equipment serviced, task, frequency, duration, outages, availability, reliability (per ATSS reporting); requirements for task performance (per specifications in rules and manuals); hours, overtime, shift; travel; allowances (per human resources data systems)
  - Data Collection Issues—methods (e.g., use of existing or subject matter experts' estimates, historic data, or data from conducting direct time study), availability of necessary data, cost and ease of data collection, level of rigor in the data (e.g., viability, utility, standardization of organizational data), amount of data to collect
  - Analysis/Model Development and Selection—building person-hour to workload relationships that are statistically valid and useful, creating electronic workbooks and Web systems to use and feed various reports
  - Implementation/Maintenance—include model utilization in policy documents, incorporate into budget cycle, refine Web platform, continuous cycle for update, addition of new products/services and retirement of legacy elements, etc.
  - Model verification, validation, and acceptance procedures defined and carried out
- Stakeholder input (adequate consideration of factors from Chapter 2 should be evident)

Area 2. Structural Detail of Model

- Model Type
  - Deterministic and/or stochastic components
  - Based upon documenting an accurate foundational work site description, or a process-oriented description, of work tasks
  - Documents standard and unique work conditions and environment components to allow for variances to normal situation in terms of additives, exclusions, deviations based upon mission, environment, or technological differences
  - Modular features for ease of update/inclusion of NextGen and legacy system changes

- Input variables
    - Direct and indirect tasks captured and considered
    - Allowances and Nonavailable Time—Personal, Fatigue, Delay, Sick, Leave, Holidays, etc.
    - Treatment of travel—without double counting
    - Standby Time—thoughtful capture and analysis
    - Fixed requirements such as specifications and/or dictated crew size (e.g., usually safety-driven, as in the "two person" rule)
    - Detail of shift analysis and post staffing, to include treatment of peaks to handle contingency-based work, risk, identification of standby time, along with review of flexibility to do training and deferrable tasks within the standby
- Output variables
    - Estimates needed for entire workforce or subcategories; types of organization, skills, and totals by location, facility, or other category
    - Not only gross FTE estimates but also ability to predict workforce needs by skill area

Area 3. Quality Factors
- Transparency
- Scalability
- Usability
- Relevance
- Validity

Area 4. Performance
- Estimate expected availability rate as function of staffing
- Estimate the cost of various levels of service or risk
- Estimate changes in levels of service and consequence
- Review and address these three issues:
    - Use of overtime
    - Work backlogs
    - Use of shortcuts
- Examine NAS redundancies
- Link to the agency's performance metrics

4

FAA Approaches to Estimating Staffing of Airway Transportation Systems Specialists

Chapter 4 examines how well the existing staffing models for the Federal Aviation Administration (FAA) Air Traffic Organization—namely, the Windows Staffing Standards Analysis System (WSSAS), the Tech Ops District Model, and the new approach planned by the Grant Thornton study team—comport with the modeling philosophy and criteria developed in Chapter 3. The aim of all three models was, and is, to help the FAA define its needs for accurate and timely staffing. The committee reviews the existing two models and the Grant Thornton approach by comparing them against the criteria identified in Chapter 3 to evaluate how well they meet the needs of the FAA. Next, alternative approaches from other domains, including the U.S. Air Force, FAA Air Traffic Control, and other countries, are discussed as additional potential sources for alternative and perhaps better models.

This review provides information regarding the desirable and undesirable features of existing staffing models and lessons learned from them. The comparison between the two FAA Airway Transportation Systems Specialists (ATSS) staffing models and their evaluation against explicit, documented criteria together provide a logical basis for future approaches that are likely to lead to valid models with practical utility for both staffing level decisions and allocations of a predetermined staff level to sites and tasks. The committee has highlighted those aspects of existing models that provide useful data and techniques, to aid the FAA in building on existing capabilities.

The committee drew on a number of sources for its evaluation of the various models, including FAA reports of evaluations of the two existing models (Grant Thornton, 2011), users' and technical guides to the WSSAS model (FAA, 2012g), and a final recommendations report on the existing models and proposed approach, written by Grant Thornton (2012). These written sources were supplemented by briefings from relevant personnel at FAA, Professional Aviation Safety Specialists (PASS), and Grant Thornton, interviews with FAA management and Grant Thornton, interviews with PASS leadership, and stakeholder input via a public invitation to comment on the project via an Internet website (see Chapter 2). Another major resource was the committee members' own expertise in modeling, human-systems integration (HSI), industrial and systems engineering, organizational psychology, economics, and operations research and their experience in industry, aviation, the U.S. Air Force, and the Department of Defense. Two technical papers on queuing models of ATSS maintenance tasks and their staffing

(Hecht and Handal, 2001; Hecht et al., 1998) provided data on the feasibility of stochastic modeling and outcome prediction in this domain. The enabling legislation for the current study specified that the resulting report to Congress be completed within 1 year; this time constraint precluded the committee from gaining hands-on experience with the two existing systems, as neither of them is currently in use or projected for future use.

HISTORY OF FAA MODELING EFFORTS FOR ATSS STAFFING

The existing staffing models and the Grant Thornton approach are briefly described here as the basis for more detailed examination and assessment in subsequent sections.

WSSAS Staffing Model

The WSSAS staffing model, which was developed in the late 1980s and early 1990s, is an updated, Microsoft Windows–based version (using the Microsoft Access database management system) of an earlier MS-DOS-based program. The two factors driving staffing demand in the model are (1) the number and types of equipment maintained, and (2) the time required to maintain the equipment. The WSSAS model is based on a synthesis of the required maintenance times for each piece of equipment in the inventory (Grant Thornton, 2011). Original data on times required for both routine and nonroutine maintenance come from direct time studies conducted by the FAA or studies conducted by contractors as part of the development of each piece of equipment. Times for each task are totaled across each unit, with allowances added for travel time, nonavailable time, and indirect work. An overhead allowance is also added to cover "technical and program support." Many reports from the model are available to managers, but the two most frequently discussed in committee meetings were the "Book 2A" and "Book 2B" reports. The Book 2A report gives overall staffing levels for each unit for current and previous years, with the added allowances. Book 2B provides a further staffing breakdown by ATSS specialties (FAA, 2012g). WSSAS is a complex model that requires considerable input data on a regular basis to provide managers with useful information regarding staffing levels. There were no data on reliability or validity of staffing predictions of this model, although users appeared to trust its outputs.

Tech Ops District Staffing Model

The Tech Ops District Model was developed in 2006 and updated in 2007 as an alternative to WSSAS.[1] It is a regression model based on then-existing staffing levels and six high-level input variables, including a number of large Terminal Radar Approach Control (TRACON) facilities. Its basic premise is that the overall 6,100 staffing level (with an annual 2.5 percent reduction in head count based on "expected efficiencies") is an exogenously determined (i.e., set by others without regard to the findings of a model) staffing level that is not subject to change through staffing model analyses. The model uses six predictors of district-level workload requirements, derived from a larger set of potential workload predictors. The regression was constructed based on 38 districts and accounted for more than 93 percent of workload variability in the dataset. All six coefficients were positive and statistically significant, which are necessary conditions for a structurally sound model as well as a valid one.[2] Output from the Tech

[1] *Tech Ops Models: WSSAS and District Model*. Personal communication from the FAA to the Committee on Staffing Needs of Systems Specialists in Aviation, November 29, 2012.

[2] Rich McCormick, director, Labor Analysis, FAA, data from unpublished 2006 "Technical Workforce Staffing and Training Plan."

Ops District Model gives the staffing levels for each district or unit. The Tech Ops District Model is simpler than the WSSAS model and requires fewer data inputs to produce outputs in each time period.

Staffing Approach by Grant Thornton–Led Study Team

In April 2011, Grant Thornton was commissioned by the FAA to bring together a team, including representatives from PASS and FAA management. This team assessed the WSSAS and Tech Ops models and began to develop a new approach. In a presentation to the committee, FAA representatives noted that "presently, staffing decisions are based on management's assessment" rather than formal models.[3] The assessment of the two current models by Grant Thornton (2011) was designed to influence the design of new models, based on the best features of existing models, to better serve the staffing needs of ATSS. A design based on this assessment is now being studied (Grant Thornton, 2012), although bids for development have not been solicited and the new model is not intended to be completed before developers can take advantage of any recommendations in this National Research Council report.

Based on their review of the FAA historical models, Grant Thornton has proposed an alternative approach, which is the subject of this section. Their methodology builds on the positive aspects of the WSSAS. Staffing demand is estimated from the amount and type of equipment supporting the National Airspace System (NAS) and the time necessary to maintain each component. The validity of the WSSAS (and consequently its predictive ability) was questioned by Grant Thornton because of questions regarding the data capture and the integrity of the data inputs used in the model. Because the main causes for concern with existing models were seen to be validity of data capture and lack of prediction ability, an improved approach should address these concerns (Grant Thornton, 2011). Note that "predictive ability" as used by Grant Thornton means the ability to accurately estimate changes in staffing levels as new equipment enters the NAS. The WSSAS model did not do that very well because of weaknesses in the data.

To improve the predictive ability of a new model, Grant Thornton made three suggestions: (1) Place greater emphasis on testing and using valid data with improved data collection processes, potentially from currently collected sources such as the Facility, Service, and Equipment Profile (FSEP), Remote Monitoring and Logging System (RMLS), and Labor Distribution Reporting (LDR). (2) Use WSSAS as a solid basis for testing a new, predictive model's results in real situations, to evaluate the new model's accuracy. (3) Produce reports in a format understandable to the different end users. Such an approach could use stakeholder analysis (i.e., the systematic collection of the needs of the various stakeholders for the model) to determine explicit model requirements, collect the necessary data, plan and develop the model, and evaluate the model results against data. Stakeholder analysis describes the HSI process of determining what those who have to interact with the model (input, analysis, and output) require to have the model meet their job needs. Neither WSSAS nor a model constructed by the proposed (to date) Grant Thornton methodology would be able to predict the performance consequences of staffing at various levels.

[3]Rich McCormick, director, Labor Analysis, FAA, presentation to the Committee on Staffing Needs of Systems Specialists in Aviation, October 19, 2012.

COMPARISON BETWEEN CURRENT AND PAST MODELS

To provide a sound basis for recommendations on future ATSS staffing models, the committee compared in detail the characteristics of each of the above models and compared each model with the criteria for valid staffing models provided in Chapter 3. The main headings of Table 4-1 are the four criteria areas of Box 3-2: Logical Design Process, Structural Detail, Quality, and Performance. To provide a succinct comparison that can guide future modeling efforts, Table 4-1 shows the relevant characteristics of the compared models as rows, with the three models as columns. Committee findings and conclusions on each of the three models are presented in the subsections below.

Findings and Conclusions on WSSAS

The WSSAS model was based on valid structure and suitable types of data and data sources. Essentially, WSSAS incorporated the pieces of equipment at each site, the number of technician hours required for each corrective or preventive maintenance action on each piece of equipment, and the probability of failure for each type of equipment. These measures were combined to establish the maintenance workload for each piece of equipment, and workloads were summed across all equipment at the site. Allowances were added for technician unavailability (e.g., training, leave, travel, etc.), and a factor was added for other required activities (indirect productive activities, including time at meetings, recordkeeping, housekeeping, etc.). Time data came from time studies and consensus judgments of subject matter experts, supplemented by contractor-provided times for new equipment. Neither the reliability of input data to the model nor the validity of the output staffing levels was measured.

WSSAS was a deterministic model; in other words, the effects of unpredictable events were not factored into the model. The reports generated were useful to supervisors and administrators, and the model was reasonably transparent to all users. The model has been updated continually since its development; however, it has not been used recently. There was never an intention to validate WSSAS against outcome measures such as NAS equipment availability.

Finding 4-1: The WSSAS model does not appear to contain stochastic elements in places where these may have been appropriate.

Conclusion 4-1: The approach represented by the original WSSAS model included many of the important variables (e.g., equipment counts and task durations together with failure rates and allowances) to determine the staffing required at each site.

Finding 4-2: The WSSAS model made no prediction of outcomes such as the impact of staffing levels on NAS availability and safety.

Findings and Conclusions on the Tech Ops District Model

The Tech Ops District Model was an allocation model only (a model aimed at distributing available resources effectively, irrespective of their collective adequacy), rather than a sufficiency model (a model designed to predict the resources needed to sustain system performances at an acceptable level). Thus, it is not an appropriate basis for moving forward toward a valid model for determining staffing requirements. It is a nonmeasurement regression model that only shows, at best, how a number of variables are related in a statistical manner to then-current staffing levels by district. The Tech Ops District Model was not validated against outcome measures and is restricted by the fixed number of employees (i.e., 6,100). It does not have the capability to predict numbers needed based on goals of safety and performance.

TABLE 4-1 Structure and Evaluation of Current and Proposed Staffing Models for ATSS

	WSSAS	Tech Ops District Model	Grant Thornton Approach
Logical Design Process			
Comprehensive Design Captures major workload drivers	Uses number and types of equipment with estimates of task duration for each, plus allowances using an algorithm described in WSSAS User Manual (Grant Thornton, 2012).	Uses a regression model where dependent variable is workload staffing. Rather than the tasks themselves, six high-level determinants of workload are the independent variables.	Plans to use number and types of equipment with estimates of task duration for each, plus allowances. Key parameters will be estimated largely in the same way as the WSSAS model.
Stakeholder Input Based on needs of all users	No data on the stakeholder input were available for this historic model.	Regression-based to give rapid assessment and minimize input. User input not specifically stated to committee.	Plans to gather input from stakeholders as basis for structure, inputs, and outputs.
Structural Detail			
Model Type Additive components vs. regression	Deterministic, additive task-based components based upon number and types of systems maintained and measured or estimated person-hours required to maintain each. Model applies allowances to account for time spent on nonmaintenance activities and generates staffing requirements.	Multi-variable regression of existing workforce in baseline year against existing drivers. The regression model identifies the predictor variables within a district that directly impact staffing and uses these variables to estimate staffing at the district level. This is actually an allocation model, because no true measurement was performed.	The proposed approach is deterministic and additive, closely linked to the WSSAS model. It follows the basic driver of the WSSAS model: equipment inventory and time for maintenance of that equipment. It is deterministic in that corrective maintenance is not considered stochastically but is based on historical, deterministic time requirements (Grant Thornton, 2012).

Input Variables Uses all significant inputs	Captures equipment types and task durations plus travel times; accommodates other FTE consumption through use of allowances.	Not based on true measurement of hours required to perform duties, detailed equipment counts, or tasks. No coverage of allowances. Variables used[a]: • **District needs** = Number of technical workforce employees needed in the district. • **Maximum hours available.** • **Number of commissioned and noncommissioned,** nonreportable facilities, services, and equipment. • **Number** of Air Route Traffic Control Centers (ARTCCs), Large TRACON facilities, national network centers.	Plans use of equipment types and task durations, plus travel times. Intended inputs: • **New categories of work.** Change from 3 (recurring, nonrecurring, allowances) to 7 (maintenance, monitor and control, other duties, admin, nonrecurring, travel, allowances) (Grant Thornton, 2012). • **Adjustment factors.** Nonstandard 2 person, environmental, work area type. • **New workload assessment** process to determine level of effort (Grant Thornton, 2012). • **Improved Precommission Facility File (PFF)** for estimating new staffing requirements as a function of equipment changes.
Output Variables Produces all required outputs	Variety of reports as WSSAS outputs, synchronized to the FAA's budget cycle. Book 2A and Book 2B were most frequently cited as useful outputs. Book 2A report gives overall staffing levels for each unit for current and previous years with the added allowances. Book 2B provides a further staffing breakdown by ATSS specialties. Outputs include estimations of needed overhead (FAA, 2012g:4).	Gives District-level staffing based on 2005-2006 levels and planned 2.5% per year overall staffing reduction.	Plans to use stakeholder input to guide appropriate outputs. Will be Web-based and use WSSAS outputs as the basis for required outputs. Plans to apply an organization-specific version of overhead within the model for District, Service Area, and National reports. District personnel noted that their definition of overhead includes administrative personnel, supervisors, and potentially program support. At FAA headquarters, Technical Support and additional levels of management are included (Grant Thornton, 2012).

continued

TABLE 4-1 Continued

	WSSAS	Tech Ops District Model	Grant Thornton Approach
Sources of Data Subject-matter expert estimates vs. current staffing vs. time study (see Chapter 3 for discussion of time estimates)	Relied on direct time study data for durations, Supplemented by estimates gathered by experienced analysts. Other data collected from systems fed by a combination of technicians who performed maintenance, data personnel at facilities, and management. Uses the following data-specific sources[a]: • **FSEP**—identifies type of equipment/services, specific configuration of the equipment and its location; predicts new equipment and decommissioning of old equipment. • **Cost centers** (facility). • **Staffing values file**—workload level of effort for each configuration of equipment. • **Categories of work—**recurring, nonrecurring, and allowances.	Data gathered from sources readily available at higher management and staff levels. Specific data sources are as above, namely: • **District needs**—Number of technical workforce employees needed in the district. • **Maximum hours available.** • **Number of commissioned and noncommissioned,** nonreportable facilities, services, and equipment. • **Number of** ARTCC, large TRACON facilities, and national network centers.	Data sources are improved versions of the following FAA systems (Grant Thornton, 2012): **FSEP** with improved PFF to better predict future demand. **RMLS** is used for logging and tracking maintenance and has several components: • logging/tracking tool • reporting tool • scheduling tool • log for outages and maintenance events. **LDR** is FAA system for logging time worked on specific activities. System has several known weaknesses, but it can at least be used reliably to account for leave allowances. **eLearning Management System** for tracking training; will be suitable as input for training allowance.
Quality			
Usability Easy to use and update	Output reports were assessed as meeting users' needs. Updated through adding data on new equipment and revising data on current equipment as physical equipment and processes changed. New time studies rarely performed. System fell out of use largely because of difficulty of updating.	Easy to use, but output of limited value to users.	Usability not yet measured, but good process should be followed for obtaining user input at design stage. Uses archival data sets already being collected so should be easier than WSSAS to update. A likely improvement over WSSAS in that it will be centrally updated and maintained.

Staffing Validity Predicts staffing levels perceived to be appropriate	Was widely seen by users as giving sensible staffing levels until it became outdated. • FSEP data should be used to identify current NAS systems, subsystems, equip and services in the new model.[a] • FSEP not as accurate in predicting out-year additions, deletions, and modifications to systems, equipment, and services due to cumbersome modifications to model required because of PFF data limitations. • Some perception that the model may have been generous or overstaffed, as levels predicted were rarely fully funded and yet mission objectives still appeared to be met.	Assumed then-current District staffing levels. This model only redistributed resources based on ratio of current workforce to various workload predictors. Also forced a 2.5% per year decrease in available resources per year on assumption that undocumented efficiencies would be achieved.	Validity in the context of the plans for this model includes tests to ensure that staffing equation code is without error, works as intended, and incorporates *a priori* validity of subject matter experts. There is no validation in the sense of a prediction that is compared to a realized value for staffing consequences. The plans indicate better prediction of new staffing demands with improvements in the PFF.
Transparency Ease of understanding	Widely accepted by administrators and users as transparent basis for workload planning because of logical structure of equipment counts, performance times, and allowances.	Not task-based, thus not transparent to final users.	Aims for understandable formulation based on task durations for each equipment type, plus allowances. Similar to WSSAS.
Scalability Can be aggregated at various levels	Can be scaled down to level of individual specialty and scaled up to district and national levels.	District-based only. Would require new regression to aggregate at higher levels or to decompose to individual specialty level.	Designed to aggregate at necessary levels, similar to WSSAS. Plans to go down to level of individual specialty and be aggregated to district and national levels.
Performance			
Consequence Validity Predicts safety and throughput outcomes	None. No consequences on system availability or maintenance backlogs are predicted, and thus WSSAS was never tested for validity.	None.	Outputs will not include consequences of staffing such as maintenance backlogs or expected system availability rates.

[a]*Tech Ops Models: WSSAS and District Model*. Personal communication from the FAA to the Committee on Staffing Needs of Systems Specialists in Aviation, November 29, 2012.

Any work regression model, without measurement of actual hours required to perform the task, will necessarily preserve the status quo in terms of the staffing level that is input to the regression. Therefore, the performance consequences of the output distribution of staffing cannot be assessed with the model and may not meet current or future performance requirements. The committee advises against the Tech Ops District Model as a source of either framework or data for future work, and this report does not consider it further as a basis for FAA staffing models.

Finding 4-3: The Tech Ops District Model was an allocation model and not a sufficiency staffing model.

Conclusion 4-2: The Tech Ops District Model is not an adequate framework for future work.

Findings and Conclusions on the Grant Thornton Approach

The design proposed by Grant Thornton for a staffing model appears to be an extension of past efforts. The Grant Thornton approach builds on the WSSAS model but suggests improvements to the key data sources for the future model. It appears to capture the relationships between equipment and maintenance staffing, and it has provisions for idiosyncratic factors (variances) affecting staffing.

Although the Grant Thornton design represents distinct improvements over WSSAS, the committee has two concerns with an approach built on the basis of the WSSAS model. First, corrective maintenance in the ATSS job often occurs in an unscheduled, stochastic manner, and the WSSAS model does not account for the intrinsically stochastic nature of these events. Even if some elements like mean time between component failures can be predicted, some randomness or unpredictability related to the timing and location of a specific failure requiring corrective maintenance remains. Before dismissing various probabilistic aspects of maintenance work and methods, these stochastic elements and their relationship to adequate and safe staffing levels need to be understood and thoroughly explored to determine if and how they should be included in the model design.

Second, like the WSSAS and Tech Ops District Models, the proposed model does not predict the consequences or results of staffing at alternative levels. It would be advisable to gather data necessary to study stochastic properties of outages, required time to repair, and shift profile dynamics mentioned in Chapter 3. It would also be helpful to explore potential linkages of key internal Technical Operations performance metrics to various levels of staffing allocations.

Finding 4-4: The Grant Thornton prospective model builds on the earlier WSSAS model, and thus inherits some of its strengths and limitations. Its strengths include the same elemental data structure, supplemented with more recent data partly derived from existing data bases.

Conclusion 4-3: Based on the latest description of the proposed model in the Grant Thornton report, the limitation of the Grant Thornton approach is the plan for a deterministic model that does not consider the implications of stochastic elements. Further, it makes no predictions of outcome measures such as NAS equipment availability and safety.

There are a number of criteria based on the committee's analysis from Chapter 3 that both the WSSAS model and the proposed Grant Thornton approach meet. Both of these models are task-based, using counts of equipment to be maintained and times required to maintain each piece as key inputs for a task. They also include allowances and variances to take account of indirect work, such as meeting attendance, paperwork, and administrative time, as well as travel time variances. They are solid logical models with only two omissions from the criteria in Chapter 3: (1) Neither of the models has a stochastic component to capture the inherent variability of task times. (2) Neither model's outputs are directly related to risk factors or overall NAS performance and safety. If the FAA were not concerned with these two issues, then the proposed model would be adequate.

POTENTIAL ALTERNATIVE MODELING APPROACHES

Before starting a major effort in model development, organizations commonly look to models that are in use in analogous situations elsewhere, both internal and external to the organization. These working, analogous models can provide a reasonable basis for evaluating approaches to new model development, as well as insights and lessons learned from others' experiences. In the case of staffing models, an existing model that is both accepted and used within the organization can be an important starting point for the development and design of a new model.

Within the FAA, staffing models are used for at least two other job series—en route air traffic controllers (see National Research Council, 2010) and aviation safety inspectors (see National Research Council, 2006). The committee examined these FAA models for insight into model development processes that have worked in the past to give FAA management and staff useful models for staffing the organization. The committee notes that Section 608 of the Federal Aviation Administration (FAA) Modernization and Reform Act of 2012 mandates a study of air traffic control staffing, with an approximate completion date of mid-2014. However, that study is running in parallel with this study, and findings from it are not yet available.

The committee sought models from organizations that have a workforce similar to the ATSS workforce. Specifically, the committee attempted to review models from the Canadian and German equivalents of the FAA, and from the U.S. Air Force.

Other FAA Staffing Models

An effort within the FAA's Office of Aviation Safety (AVS) organization resulted in creation of model criteria for staffing standards for the aviation safety inspector workforce (National Research Council, 2006). The committee understands that the AVS Staffing Tool and Reporting System (ASTARS) includes a predictive model for both the safety technical specialist workforce and the operational support workforce. ASTARS provides specific modeling equations for position types (e.g., operations inspectors, maintenance inspectors). The model considers the complexity requirements of specific jobs (based on factors such as the size of the fleet being inspected, the variety of aircraft type for which a specific inspector is responsible, and the experience levels of the maintenance staff subject to inspection). The committee understands that the FAA is also expanding the use of LDR data in ASTARS. The use of LDR data was considered problematic for the AVS workforce in the past because of reporting inconsistencies among the aviation safety inspectors personnel and limited categories for reporting certain types of tasks (National Research Council, 2006), and this committee has heard similar concerns from the ATSS workforce, as discussed in Chapter 2. If the AVS organization has now overcome those concerns about LDR, understanding their process could help the Technical Operations organization as it develops its models. Regardless of the use of the LDR for data input, the parallels between the AVS organization and the Technical Operations organization make the AVS model criteria a useful source for modeling processes in Technical Operations.

U.S. Air Force Staffing Models

The U.S. Air Force has employed teams of manpower analysts to create staffing models for many years. Currently, the Air Force Manpower Division of the Air Force Personnel Center (formerly the Air Force Manpower Agency) provides Air Force officials at all levels with the tools to identify essential personnel resources required for the effective and efficient accomplishment of the Air Force mission. These tools are used to program personnel resources and are used as the foundational target for accessing, training, assigning, and utilizing Air Force personnel resources. Air Force representatives presented the committee with an overview briefing of their modeling and requirements determination process. Because the Air Force includes a number of occupations that are similar to the ATSS job series in the FAA, the committee spent substantial time reviewing the models that the Air Force uses to establish staffing standards for some of those occupations.

These models included Air Force Manpower Standards (AFMS) for Ground Radio Maintenance (AFMS 38AC), Meteorological and Navigation Systems Equipment Maintenance (AFMS 38AA), and Air Traffic Control and Landing Systems Radar Maintenance (AFMS 38AB) (see U.S. Air Force, 1998, 1995b, 1994, respectively). Each of these models quantifies the manpower required to accomplish the tasks described in a detailed process-oriented description for varying levels of workload. The AFMS outline specific core team requirements and predict personnel resource needs based upon counts of specific equipment sets or equipment equivalents, multiplied by a measurement of personnel-hours required to maintain the various end-items. Several of the models contain variances for factors such as extended travel distances, unique equipment, corrosion control, seasonal storm days, and snow and ice removal. The instructions outline application of various allowances and factors and refer the reader to tables that show the FTEs required by skill specialty and grade.

Although the Air Force has used these specific models for an extended time, the committee understands that new process-oriented models are currently under development, some of which may combine existing methods with process modeling techniques. The models the committee reviewed are similar in process, structure, and output to the FAA's WSSAS model.

The Air Force employs the Logistics Composite Model (LCOM) program to identify the manpower positions required to perform many aircraft maintenance activities. It is now a SIMSCRIPT[4] model that can run on many current desktop PCs, with many tailored versions built for specific weapon systems and scenarios. The LCOM simulation model integrates stochastic features such as queuing, Markovian processes, and vast amounts of available maintenance data to support a wide range of investigations into resourcing, skills required, staffing levels, performance, and consequences. Several iterations of the Air Force staffing models are usually run to help establish suitable outputs for creating staffing scenarios, which are often tied to peacetime or wartime utilization of the aircraft fleet.

Other Potentially Relevant Models

Although the committee requested detailed modeling information from NavCanada and Deutsche Flugsicherung, the Canadian and German counterparts to the American FAA, these private organizations were not able to release any formal documentation concerning their proprietary staffing models.

[4]According to the website dictionary.com, SIMSCRIPT is a free-form, English-like general-purpose simulation language produced by Harry Markowitz and colleagues at RAND Corporation in 1963. It was implemented as a FORTRAN preprocessor for the IBM 7090 mainframe computer and was designed for large discrete simulations. It influenced Simula. Later versions included SIMSCRIPT I.5 and SIMSCRIPT II.5.

Another potential source for modeling assistance could be from industry modelers such as those in the aircraft maintenance sector whose models are proprietary and could not be viewed by the committee.

A LOGICAL APPROACH TO A NEW MODEL FOR ATSS

The search for alternative approaches to staffing models from other enterprises also provided some insights that largely confirm that a detailed deterministic modeling approach in the near term, with perhaps a later, more dynamic (stochastic) modeling approach, would be worthwhile and useful if feasible. The FAA's modeling efforts based on the 2006 report on staffing models for aviation safety inspectors (National Research Council, 2006) resulted in the ASTARS model, which has been used to help determine 2014 and 2015 staffing requirements (FAA, 2012f). The en route air traffic controllers' model developed by Mitre's Center for Advanced Aviation System Development (National Research Council, 2010) has been used in staffing of the en route centers except for those in Anchorage, Guam, and San Juan and the Oceanic areas of New York and Oakland. Both of these FAA models and those used by various parts of the Air Force are largely in line with the committee's criteria discussed in Chapter 3 and summarized in Box 3-2.

The committee concluded from its analysis that the approach suggested by Grant Thornton was likely to be successful if implemented because it is based on the logically sound approach of the WSSAS model, rather than on the Tech Ops District allocation model. The WSSAS model was correctly based on the counts of each equipment type at each location and on the times required for the different maintenance needs of those pieces of equipment. In addition, the proposed Grant Thornton approach would be easier to maintain because it would use data capture from a number of existing sources to supplement the proposed new time study data. Thus, its continuing data requirements would potentially be less onerous than those of WSSAS, decreasing the risk that the new model would fall into disuse from lack of updating as NAS equipment and maintenance requirements change over time. The committee notes, however, that direct time studies can only measure durations of observable tasks. As work becomes less physical and more cognitive, task durations become more difficult to measure because fewer observable actions delineate their boundaries. It is still possible to measure overall task durations using time study, but component elements may not be as clear.

However, the committee has two potential concerns with the proposed model. First, as currently proposed, it is a deterministic rather than stochastic model, even though it is known that time between failures and times for maintenance do vary, often considerably. Second, it predicts only staffing outcomes rather than true performance outcomes. The committee believes it is worthwhile for the FAA to consider each of these issues in more depth because they represent potential weaknesses that should be addressed at an early stage of model design. The two issues are related in that the level of service provided by the ATSS is a function of stochastic factors. In Chapter 3 the committee noted that the workload demand at any one point in time is highly variable, combining relatively predictable scheduled tasks and relatively unpredictable unscheduled tasks. The level of workload demand, when matched against the workforce available, determines the level of ATSS service accomplishment and thus the functioning of the NAS.

The NAS has great designed-in redundancy; it even has mitigations such as increased Miles-in-Trail[5] to keep traffic moving when all the redundancy is consumed. At some point though, the sheer number of tasks instantaneously requiring attention, compared to the available number of ATSS personnel, could lead to a loss of service. While much of the focus is on the nationwide staffing level, the maintenance

[5]Miles-in-Trail (MIT) restrictions are one of the most commonly used traffic management initiatives. They are most often used to manage arrival flows into airports. Traffic managers often use MIT restrictions to protect a destination airport, particularly when capacity has been reduced due to weather or during periods of high volume. They also use MIT restric-

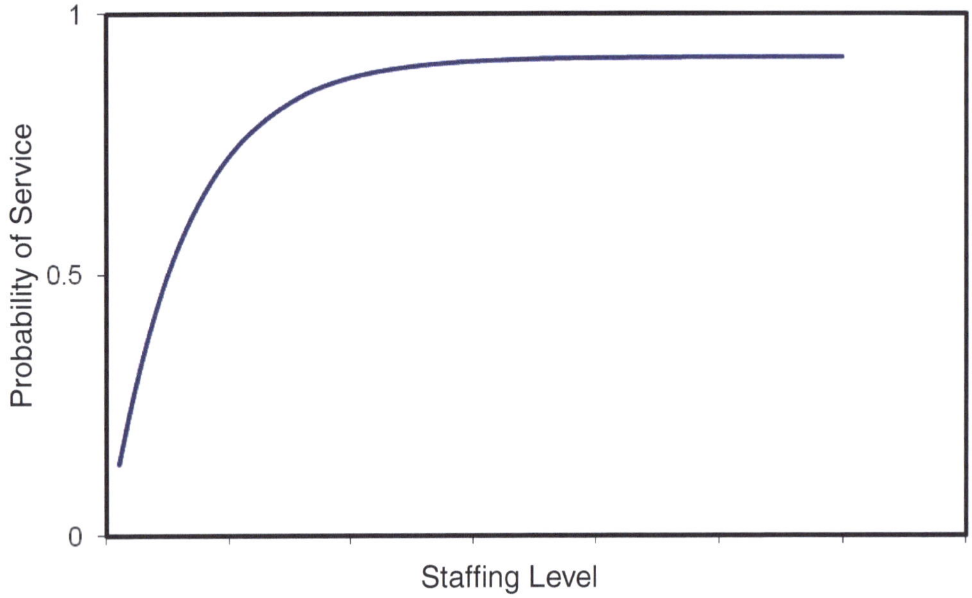

FIGURE 4-1 Conceptual logical relationship between service and staffing level. Probability of service is defined as potential availability of the NAS. It incorporates both failures and time to restore.
SOURCE: Adapted from multiple figures in Hecht et al. (1998).

system can become overwhelmed locally, even if national staffing is adequate. A truly valid model of staffing for ATSS personnel should be able to address this issue directly so that decision makers can make intelligent decisions balancing level of service and taxpayer cost at both local and national levels.

An early example relevant to ATSS is the paper by Hecht and colleagues (1998). Their model used a stochastic modeling approach with different technician skills, an exponential relationship between failure rate and duration of repair, and a valid model of redundancy to predict the consequences of different staffing levels. In this way the impact of staffing decisions on overall system performance could be quantified. Although the specific equipment levels, staffing levels, and redundancies used by Hecht and colleagues (1998) may no longer be relevant, applying their methodology is likely to result in valid models.

Better system design can increase the level of service for any given staffing level. For example, technology improvements, training improvements, or organizational improvements such as better deployment of multi-skilled ATSS personnel can increase the safety and stability of the NAS. For any given state of system design, there will be some relationship between service and staffing, generally showing increased service with increased staffing. This logical relationship is shown in Figure 4-1.

It is not the responsibility of the modelers, nor of this committee, to determine the correct tradeoff between staffing and service: defining the acceptable tradeoff is a policy role of the decision makers at the FAA and ultimately of the federal government acting in the public interest. However, the FAA should provide a model that defines the service/staffing curve with some transparency of its linkage to underlying, objective drivers of that relationship. Such a model allows for explicit decisions on appro-

tions to smooth out flows to support merging streams. (Definition found at http://www.mitre.org/work/tech_papers/tech_papers_07/06_0967 [June 2013].)

priate staffing level to meet the desired level of service and also allows for system improvements to be evaluated in terms of their impact on overall system performance.

The committee has assumed in Figure 4-1 that all instances of service denial are equal, so that probability of service is the only measure of performance or effectiveness. However, the definition of service also needs to include a dimension of severity of consequences. The same outage (e.g., of a Primary RADAR or Radio channel) has far greater consequences at a major airport or en route sector than at a regional airport. Severity measures could include the number of flights affected or even the number of near-miss or actual collisions. This finding of differential impact from the same event implies that two staffing sites requiring the same probability of service should not necessarily be equally staffed. Almost any safety management system will include the two dimensions of probability and severity in assessing risks (see Figure 3-3, as an example), so this concept is certainly not novel to the FAA.

A model incorporating both stochastic demand and stochastic ATSS staffing levels would be much more realistic than a simpler deterministic model. Such a model would also enable those responsible for staffing ATSS to show the impact of the chosen staffing levels on the measure of most direct interest to the FAA's air traffic management customers: the service level of the NAS. Whether a deterministic or a stochastic model best meets the needs of the FAA is a decision that needs to be made based on the inputs and modeling effort required in relationship to the outputs needed—and in particular the potential consequences of ignoring the stochastic relationships. That decision should not be based on cost and convenience alone.

SUMMARY AND RECOMMENDATIONS

This chapter has taken the modeling approaches and criteria developed in Chapter 3 from staffing model knowledge and has applied them to the WSSAS model, the Tech Ops District Model, and the proposed Grant Thornton approach to modeling. First, the factual basis of three models was tabulated and assessed in terms of the criteria. Next, other sources of successful modeling in similar situations were assessed for the insights they might add to the future models of ATSS staffing developed by the FAA.

The committee can summarize the attributes and the evaluation of models based on these attributes as a set of statements about what are good criteria for the FAA's future modeling efforts. The best science currently available supports the following recommendations for a valid and usable model.

Recommendation 4-1: The FAA should develop a new ATSS staffing model based on the modeling framework and criteria developed in this report. The model should be developed using a model structure that is based on equipment inventory, failure rates, and time to perform each task, and should include any valid allowances and accommodations. The model structure should include both deterministic and stochastic estimates for variables such as task duration, as appropriate. The developed model structure should be based on the different specialties of ATSS technicians, rather than providing just an overall staffing level at each facility.

Recommendation 4-2: The FAA should develop a model that captures stochastic elements, unless it can be demonstrated that stochastic aspects of the maintenance process have no material effect on the staffing. For example, some tasks may exhibit multiple deterministic durations of identifiable elements, rather than strictly stochastic durations.

Recommendation 4-3: The FAA should incorporate data for the model that are appropriate to the duration and frequency of the tasks modeled and to its data collection capabilities. Specifically, the FAA needs a process to systematically validate through direct observation both historical estimates of task durations and estimates by subject matter experts.

Recommendation 4-4: The FAA should ensure that the ongoing data collection and input essential for model use do not place an unacceptable burden on data providers.

Recommendation 4-5: The FAA should ensure that output reports from the system predict consequences such as overall NAS availability time, deferred preventive maintenance activities, and overtime required.

Recommendation 4-6: The FAA should ensure that output reports are tailored closely to the needs of FAA's internal users at multiple organizational levels, in order to increase transparency of, and user trust in, the model.

5

Implementation and Sustainability of the Staffing Model

The success of any staffing model is dependent on both the validity of the model developed and the manner in which it is implemented. The purpose of this chapter is to present and discuss both the requirements for successfully implementing a staffing model and the factors that must be considered to sustain the use of the model over time.

TIMELINE

Airway Transportation Systems Specialists (ATSS) are responsible for maintaining many types of equipment in multiple types of locations across a wide geographic area, and as discussed in previous chapters, many factors affect the staffing levels necessary to maintain the National Airspace System (NAS) effectively and safely. Consequently, any model that will accurately estimate necessary ATSS staffing levels will be complex and likely require a considerable amount of time to develop. Similarly, a complex staffing model is likely to need a great deal of preparation for implementation, ranging from testing the model to training Federal Aviation Administration (FAA) personnel to use the model, and it is likely to take a considerable amount of time to implement.

The actual time required to develop such a model should be proposed by the developer. Experts on the committee who have developed complex models estimate the development time to be between 12 and 24 months for a deterministic model and longer for a robust simulation tool like the Air Force's Logistics Composite Model. The implementation time could take 6-12 months in conjunction with the FAA's planning, programming, and budget cycle requirements. If there are significant changes to staffing at locations, these may need to be managed over a longer time through attrition, hiring lead times, etc. The FAA's 2012 contract with the Professional Aviation Safety Specialists (PASS) labor union, maintains the 6,100 ATSS staffing level as a staffing floor for 16 months (Professional Aviation Safety Specialists, 2012). If the developer's schedule estimates for model development and implementation exceed the 16-month limit, the FAA will need to determine how to manage staffing levels until the new staffing model is implemented.

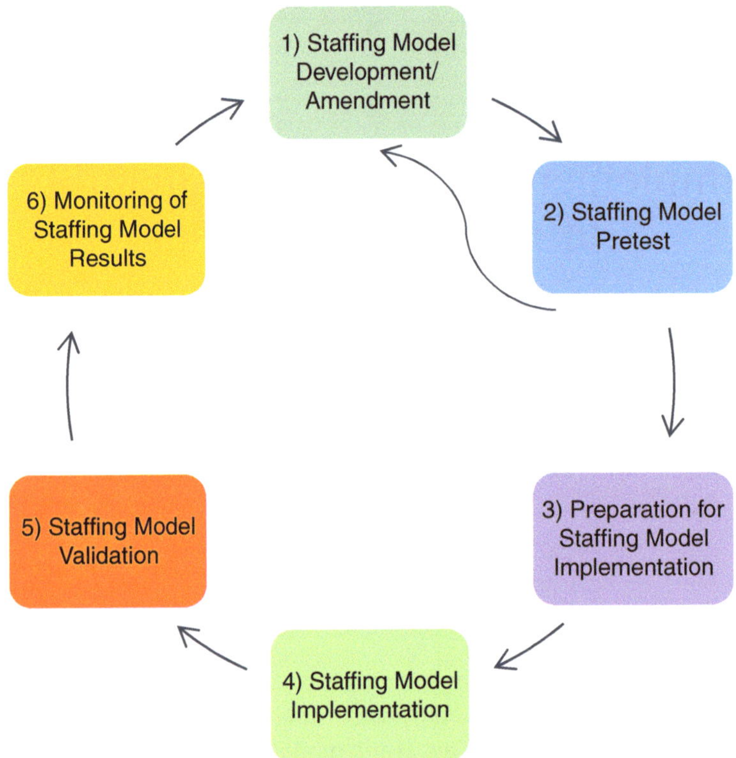

FIGURE 5-1 Phases of staffing model development and implementation.

Figure 5-1 provides a high-level overview of the major steps from model development through implementation. Each of these steps comprises a number of activities that should be undertaken to increase the likelihood of a successful model launch. Each activity requires time and resources. Ideally, the FAA and its staffing model experts would add to these major steps as needed and elaborate on each, specifying what needs to be done by whom and creating a schedule to be followed for each step.

Step 1 in Figure 5-1 includes all the activities associated with the actual development of the model that have been detailed in the preceding chapters. Specifically, Figure 3-1 in Chapter 3 details the five phases that should be incorporated into model development. Although the workforce planning process described in Chapter 3 and the implementation process discussed here in Chapter 5 overlap considerably, this discussion is meant to highlight the activities related to successful implementation.

Although much of the work falls on the shoulders of the experts designing the model, the input into the model will likely be the responsibility of FAA employees. The accuracy and the value of the results of the model are limited by the quality of that input. Inaccurate, biased, or incomplete data can skew the recommended staffing levels. Data from such time recording systems as the Labor Distribution Recording system are noted for their limitations and the unreliability of their data. Similarly, information about the time required for maintenance may be highly variable due to the age of the equipment, the amount it is used, and the environment in which it is used. The FAA staff will need to participate in activities aimed at developing processes that produce accurate information about the tasks ATSS personnel perform and the factors that affect the time required to perform them. Ideally, in the long term, the FAA would embrace information technology enterprise architecture strategies. A comprehensive enterprise architecture would encompass a visionary review and where appropriate, integration of the entire set of information technology systems that ATSS workers and their leadership find necessary for data input. Such an architecture would boost future modeling and total resource control, including control of staffing. To begin, the FAA may desire to modernize human resource, time tracking, and maintenance systems, and at the same time integrate them to achieve synergies between these systems, because they are used by the ATSS workforce, as well as to oversee and manage it.[1]

The introduction of a staffing model offers an opportunity to establish productive relationships among the people critical to developing, implementing, and using it, as well as an opportunity to create systems that interact and support each other, limiting the need for redundant inputs of the same information. The modeling experts, data experts, and ATSS functional experts could seize this opportunity to form an enduring partnership and ensure communications intended to constantly improve the model, its inputs, and its utility and usability. In addition, the need for an accurate time reporting data base that feeds the staffing model creates opportunities to improve and integrate human resource systems.

Moreover, the more that FAA employees are involved in the development process—as opposed to simply arriving one day to learn that a new staffing model is in place—the more likely they will be to provide the inputs needed to make the model work well and the more they will be to have an "ownership interest" in the model and be willing to help with the inevitable tweaking process as the model is implemented. For the employees to participate willingly, they must understand that the purpose of the model is to improve their ability to perform their jobs more efficiently and effectively, rather than, for example, to see how much the workforce can be reduced or increased.

There are numerous Safety and Risk Management protocols available today to help quantify potential risks both objectively and subjectively and then prioritize or target those risks that appear unacceptable or too great not to take proactive measures to manage them better. Current FAA Safety and Risk Management frameworks and safety metrics may provide a starting point to assist in providing guidelines to a specific modeling effort. Still, it is highly likely that a team of functional experts—to include those with significant expertise in assessing and improving safety and decreasing risk—would be useful if called on to help clarify risks inherent in processes and staffing associated with a particular study effort.

Step 2 involves a pretest of the model prior to full implementation. The purpose of this type of pretest is to identify problems with the model and its results and rectify them prior to actual model use. The basis for this evaluation is the set of quality factors described in Step 5. Because the evaluation in Step 2 is preliminary and precedes the roll-out to users, several aspects cannot be assessed. For example, usability cannot be studied directly as the ultimate users will not actually use the model prior to the Step 2 evaluation; however, pilot tests with samples of users should be encouraged.

Those who create the model need to generate a "trial model application," compare the results to current (or past) staffing levels, and collect data about the impact of the new staffing levels (whether they are higher or lower or remain the same) on the FAA's ability to maintain the NAS. For this test of the model, in addition to collecting hard data for statistical comparisons, such as number and length of outages, overtime hours, and backlog, the modelers need to prepare to collect qualitative data such as leaders' reactions to the differences between actual and proposed staffing levels.

Chapter 3 provides five criteria by which a staffing model should be evaluated: transparency, scalability, usability, relevance, and validity. The new ATSS staffing model should be compared to these standards and adapted as needed prior to implementation in Step 4. As review and improvement of the

[1]FAA NAS Enterprise Architecture. Presentation by Jesse Wjintjes, NAS chief architect, to the April 28, 2010, Meeting of Agency Chief Architects. Available: http://www.jpdo.gov/library/PartnerAgency/Jesse_Wijntjes_Briefing.pdf [May 2013].

staffing model is a continuous process, these five criteria should be kept in mind once the model is implemented and is being validated and amended.

Step 3 focuses on the activities necessary to prepare the FAA to transition from the current state of staffing to a new process for establishing staffing levels via a carefully constructed staffing model. This committee was specifically charged with considering transition in its statement of task (see Box 1-1). Because the current staffing level for ATSS personnel of 6,100 is dictated by the contract to which the FAA and PASS agreed (Professional Aviation Safety Specialists, 2012), the transition phase will not focus on changing the procedures for estimating staffing requirements and allocation of those personnel. Instead, the transition should focus on installing the new modeling system, procuring equipment (e.g., computer equipment to run the model and distribute reports), personnel, and other resources needed to execute the model, ensure reliable data inputs, and educate users.

In addition, the FAA will need to develop a detailed plan, based upon input from the employees, to *implement* the new staffing model. For example, the FAA must decide whether the staffing model should be rolled out across the country at one time or implemented region by region, determining the pros and cons to each approach and remediating as many of the disadvantages of the option chosen as possible. In addition, the FAA must develop the timeline for the transition, checking to see what other events might affect the implementation. This implementation plan also needs to contend with the implications of decreased numbers of ATSS personnel needed in some locations and increased numbers of ATSS personnel needed in other areas. Among such implications are preparing the organization for employee movement (e.g., movement of ATSS personnel from areas where their expertise is surplus to other areas where it is needed), employee redundancy, and new hiring demands. If the employee movements are significant, they can be phased in over many fiscal quarters or several years. To the extent that personnel will be moved in ways that require bargaining with the labor union representing ATSS personnel, the FAA should prepare for and fund contract negotiations with PASS. The current hiring process for ATSS personnel and the training and certification processes are lengthy. When ATSS personnel are needed in one location, the FAA must factor the hiring-training cycle into its plans. Although the task may be daunting, the FAA might also consider improvements to the new hire processes as it develops and implements a new staffing model.

In addition, the transition plan should include training of both the staff who execute the model and all the managers and ATSS technicians who are affected by it. A new staffing model should be developed by model experts in partnership with functional experts and staff. It will be an essential requirement of implementation to train those who will use it so that all levels can use the reporting mechanisms of the model. Because of the number of users and their varied needs, training FAA personnel in how to use the system and interpret the output that is relevant to their work will not be a trivial undertaking, and the personnel necessary to develop and provide the training, as well as support ongoing usage of the modeling system, must be funded.

The model is likely to be better accepted if affected personnel (i.e., ATSS personnel and their managers) are informed of how the model works. This is part of transparency, one of the quality criteria from the 2006 report, *Staffing Standards for Aviation Safety Inspectors* (National Research Council, 2006). An understanding of the statistical intricacies of the model is probably not necessary for most employees; however, an overview of the input and the considerations that the model takes into account will help managers and ATSS personnel see how numbers are derived, appreciate the rationale behind increases and decreases in staffing levels, and understand their role in providing quality inputs into FAA data systems. This will also help FAA employees to be understanding contributors to periodic model refinements and updates—for the good of the whole team and the system they support. In addition, PASS must understand the basics of the model and support its development. Without PASS's active participation, it is unlikely that a sufficient model can be built or implemented.

Step 4 encompasses the actual implementation and rollout of the model according to the plans laid out in Step 3, all of which should logically be synchronized with key FAA human resources, training, and budget processes to the extent possible. It is a tool to help all of these systems to be more accurate and effective by defining and defending the full-time equivalent requirements needed to serve the NAS.

Step 5 is the evaluation of the quality of the staffing model against the five standards discussed in Chapter 3: relevance, scalability, transparency, usability, and validity. Once the model is implemented, the modeling team must determine how well the model and its implementation are doing on the following markers of quality:

- Relevance: Does the model capture the important drivers of workload and provide the appropriate level of detail in the output?
- Scalability: Can the results of the model be accurately aggregated at higher levels to predict staffing needs by facility, geographic region, or discipline?
- Transparency: Is the model understood by the users and those affected by it?
- Usability: Can the model be implemented and improved to make the intended staffing predictions by those who were intended to use it?
- Validity: Does the staffing level predicted match the actual need and allow the ATSS workforce to maintain the NAS safely and efficiently?

All of the quality standards are important, but validity is perhaps the most critical. Unless the results of the staffing plan allow the FAA to maintain the NAS, nothing else is relevant. Also important is the sustainability of the staffing system. If tasks associated with using the model are so laborious that they cannot be accomplished in a reasonable period of time, the modeling system is unlikely to be used and maintained regardless of its validity.

To a large extent Step 5 and Step 2 are similar. Both are designed to evaluate the model's quality. The evaluation in Step 5 is usually more extensive because it occurs after the model has been used.

Step 6 includes the activities that are necessary to sustain the model over a period of time: monitor the staffing model, evaluate its adequacy, and make adjustments as needed. The staffing model that is produced as a result of this study will be more effective if it is periodically reviewed and updated to reflect the changing environment of ATSS work.

The FAA should try to identify as many sources of information about the effectiveness of the staffing model as possible. While much information will come from the professionals who use the model to estimate and allocate ATSS personnel, the FAA should consider identifying best practices from other large organizations that use staffing models, as well as creating employee suggestion programs and lessons-learned programs that encourage constructive criticism and helpful suggestions for remediation.

Both quantitative and qualitative data can inform the FAA of the strengths and weaknesses of the staffing model. Hard data such as outages, overtime, and inspection and preventive maintenance backlogs relate to the ultimate criterion: maintaining staffing at levels necessary to keep the NAS safe and efficient. Qualitative data such as supervisors' perspectives on revised staffing levels, including the effect on employee fatigue and morale, can also help to evaluate the effectiveness of the model as well as detect unintended consequences from applying it.

Note that the implementation cycle begins again after Step 6. As results from the FAA's ongoing evaluation against the five quality standards indicate where amendments are needed to the staffing model, modifications should be made and the cycle of implementation should begin anew. An effective and useful modeling process takes into account the lessons that have accrued from each round of the implementation process and incorporates them into the next iteration of the staffing model, resulting in a spiral development process. During this cycle, one change related to the modeling parameters may be the result of several changes related to the work performed by ATSS personnel. For example, by using the model through one staffing cycle, the modelers and the users of the model may learn that certain forms of data are not reliable enough to produce sufficiently accurate estimates of staffing needs. The inaccuracy of the data may be the result of aging equipment that demands varying amounts of time for maintenance and repair. At the same time, the quality of the data may be affected by the time recording system. Thus, changes to the model may be based on the retirement of legacy equipment as well as revisions to the time recording systems currently in use. The timelines for each step of the process are different across organizations and depend on multiple factors such as the variability of the job across locations and functions, complexity of the model designed, the number of people who provide information or must be informed, the resources available, the capabilities of the contractor who develops the model, and other factors. Nevertheless, an important first step in the design of a staffing model project will be to create a timeline that specifies the amount of time to be devoted to each stage of the project.

Recommendation 5-1: The FAA should prepare a timeline that details all the activities associated with model development and implementation that must be completed and should ensure that the resources necessary to accomplish each are available.

Recommendation 5-2: Once implemented, the FAA should continue to monitor the effectiveness of the staffing model by collecting data from multiple sources and should make adjustments as needed to enhance the accuracy of the model. In addition, the model should be adapted as changes to the major components of the model are made, such as changes in the tasks performed, equipment used, and training processes.

In addition to testing the model and engaging in continuous improvement activities, there are several critical elements related to implementation: the FAA staff who will administer the staffing model; equipment and other resources; and funding for all aspects of the model including consultants, equipment, FAA staff, training, and other costs. These critical elements are briefly discussed below.

FAA STAFF

FAA employees will be involved in the development and implementation of a staffing model in a variety of roles. Even when experts employed by a vendor develop a complex staffing model, the FAA needs to provide staff to guide the project and facilitate access to appropriate data and information to support the development work. Unless the FAA staff provides input, or assigns functional experts to periodically work with or as part of the modeling effort, the model that is created is not likely to take into account accurately the important factors that affect staffing levels and to reflect actual staffing needs.

Similarly, FAA employees are likely to be involved in the actual execution of the model to establish staffing levels. Again, even if significant work associated with the implementation is contracted to a vendor, the FAA staff still needs to supply the input to the model, to ensure its accuracy and its thoroughness. The FAA will need to plan for these positions and take the steps necessary to ensure they are filled with personnel with the appropriate knowledge, skills, and abilities.

Finally, the FAA staff provides the necessary continuity and historical knowledge for keeping the model current and transparent. Without knowledge of how the model was built and has changed over time, the use of any model becomes a mere rote procedure, performed ritually rather than used for its original and important purpose.

In addition to the creation and actual execution of the model, there are other tasks that should be performed during the implementation phase. For example, training of the managers and ATSS personnel who are affected by the new staffing model will require training personnel who are able to explain both the model and the implications of its use, not just the mechanics of input and output.

EQUIPMENT AND OTHER RESOURCES

In addition to personnel, other resources related to the implementation of the staffing model include the computer systems necessary to run the models. The 2012 Grant Thornton report recommends a Web-based system that allows for broad access and facilitates system updates (Grant Thornton, 2012:28). For example, the Web-based system should allow multiple, simultaneous users while maintaining control of the processes centrally. Modules that can be turned on or off, removed, and replaced will contribute to the flexibility of a complex modeling system. Ideally, the Web-based system is updated continuously via links to data feeds from other FAA systems. For example, a data base that maintains records of maintenance events, repairs, time spent, travel time, etc., could automatically feed and update the staffing model and revise predictions. Development of this system would need to be funded and implemented as part of the model development, if this choice is approved.

FUNDING

The investment in a staffing model is likely to be substantial. The FAA must be prepared to pay for not only the consultants who develop it but also for the information technology systems on which the resulting model is run, the FAA employees who interface with the consultants, and the training of FAA employees who use the model. Additionally, the FAA must be prepared either to fund the number of employees generated by the model or, if not funded, to clearly define and potentially live with the risks taken on. The agency should also be prepared to explain how these risks would be prioritized and mitigated. The funding requirement could be particularly challenging if the number of ATSS personnel determined from the staffing model exceeds the current staffing level of 6,100. The funding must cover not only the salaries of additional employees but also the processes by which these new employees are acquired and trained. There are also costs associated with downsizing and relocating ATSS personnel where they are needed, and these costs should be budgeted if that need arises.

The development and implementation of a staffing model will not occur in a vacuum. There are undoubtedly many other process improvements related to the ATSS job that could be pursued and that will have an effect on the ATSS personnel workload and the staffing model. The importance of human-systems integration (HSI) was discussed in Chapters 1 and 3. As the FAA improves its operations in the manpower domain of HSI, it will need to seek continued, deliberate improvement and synergy across the other eight HSI domains. As the FAA implements a new staffing model, it has an opportunity to evaluate its entire talent management system and optimize each component. For example, training and certification procedures should be considered at the same time that a new staffing model is being developed and implemented. Reducing the time to certify technicians, either through more accessible training or by the ability to certify experienced hires without travel to Oklahoma City, will affect the model's effectiveness in maintaining the efficiency and safety of the NAS.

Similarly, revising the process by which the appropriate staffing number is determined will emphasize the importance of accurate input data and encourage a revision of the processes by which ATSS personnel's time is tracked, equipment inventoried, spare parts for the NAS maintained, etc. Process improvements in how maintenance work is performed are expected to be ongoing, with continuous improvements. All of these ancillary activities will also require funding in addition to what has been allocated for the modeling effort.

This report has noted repeatedly the importance of informing ATSS and PASS about the new model and explaining how it was developed, what it takes into account, how it will be implemented, etc. Funds must be available for the staff that creates written informational brochures, designs talking points, delivers this information in an understandable way, and handles the questions that will arise. Because of the importance of communications to the success of a new staffing model, professionals should be engaged to maximize the clarity and persuasiveness of the material.

CONCLUSION

The FAA is on the right track by aggressively seeking a new and appropriate manpower model. The FAA's contract with Grant Thornton is commendable (Grant Thornton, 2012), but it can be taken to a better level through deliberate analysis and inclusion of stochastic and performance dimensions in modeling a required workforce, even as the ATSS workforce takes on the challenge of maintaining the NAS in the coming decades. The 2-year process that FAA has already undertaken to assess its current models and data systems and to plan ways to improve its data systems should facilitate model development and implementation.

Ideally, the FAA will institute a rigorous implementation process for the new staffing model and related processes and will embark on the journey of continuous improvement. In the future, the staffing system will be regularly reviewed and improved at the same time as other process improvements that will increase both the efficiency and the safety of the NAS. Implementation of a new staffing model includes a number of tasks, including activities such as acquiring computer equipment to host the model, educating users, and evaluating the model against the criteria for quality multiple times. A robust staffing model is likely to improve the process for allocating staff and contribute to the maintenance of the NAS; however, the implementation and use of that staffing model will require considerable attention and resources from the FAA on an ongoing basis.

References

Beichelt, F., and Tittmann, P. (2012). *Reliability and Maintenance: Networks and Systems.* Boca Raton, FL: Chapman and Hall/CRC.

Bisantz, A.D., and Drury, C.G. (2004). Applications of archival and obervational data. In J. Wilson, ed., *Evaluation of Human Work, Third Edition.* The Netherlands: CRC Press.

Booher, H. (2003). *Handbook of Human-Systems Integration.* Hoboken, NJ: Wiley-Interscience.

Bottino, L.J., and Hughes, W.J. (2004). *The Concept of Remote Maintenance Monitoring and its Computer Architecture.* IEEE, The 23rd Digital Avionics Systems Conference. Available: http://www.ieee.org/portal/innovate/search/article_details.html?article=1390771 [May 2013].

Capshaw, D., Dillingham, J., and Oliver, B. (2011). How to use overtime. *Industry Week: Manufacturing Leadership Excellence.* April 12. Available: http://www.industryweek.com/companies-amp-executives/how-use-overtime [May 2013].

Carson, J.S. (2002). Model verification and validation. *Proceedings of the 2002 Winter Simulation Conference, December 8-11, 2002, San Diego, CA.* J. Charnes, C.-H. Chen, J. Snowdon, and C.E. Yücesan, eds. Hanover, MD: INFORMS Simulation Society. Available: http://www.informs-sim.org/wsc02papers/008.pdf [May 2013].

Department of Commerce. (2008). *Federal Strategic Spectrum Plan.* Available: http://www.ntia.doc.gov/files/ntia/publications/federalstrategicspectrumplan2008_0.pdf [May 2013].

Department of Defense. (1993). *System Safety Program Requirements.* MIL-STD 882C. Washington, DC: U.S. Department of Defense.

Department of Defense. (2009). *DoD Modeling and Simulation (M&S) Verification, Validation, and Accreditation (VV&A).* Number 5000.61. Washington, DC: U.S. Department of Defense.

Department of Transportation. (2012). *Budget Estimates for Fiscal Year 2013. Federal Aviation Administration.* Available: http://www.faa.gov/about/office_org/headquarters_offices/apl/aatf/media/FAA_FY2013_Budget_Estimates.pdf [May 2013].

Electronic Technicians Association. (2013). *Airway Transportation Systems Specialist (Environmental) job posting.* Available: http://careers.eta-i.org/jobs/4938797/airway-transportation-systems-specialist-environmental [May 2013].

FAA (Federal Aviation Administration). (1992). *Order 1380.40C, Airway Facilities Sector Staffing Standard System.* December 21. Federal Aviation Administration, Department of Transportation. Available: http://www.faa.gov/regulations_policies/orders_notices/index.cfm/go/document.information/documentID/6953 [May 2013].

FAA. (2007a). *Air Traffic Organization Safety Management System.* Order JO 1000.37. March 19. Washington, DC: U.S. Department of Transportation. Available: http://www.faa.gov/documentLibrary/media/Order/ND/1000.37.pdf [May 2013].

FAA. (2007b). *JO 6040.15E. National Airspace Performance Reporting System.* December 31. Federal Aviation Administration, Washington, DC.

FAA. (2010). *Order 6000.15E Pocket Reference: General Maintenance Handbook for NAS Facilities*. L. Overby, ed. Washington, DC: NAS Policy Team, AJW-163, Federal Aviation Administration.

FAA. (2011a). *6000.15F. General Maintenance Handbook for National Airspace Systems (NAS) Facilities with Change 2.* Responsible Office: AJW-163, NAS Policy and Planning Services, Federal Aviation Administration, Washington, DC.

FAA. (2011b). *National Airspace System Capital Investment Plan for Fiscal Years 2013-2017*. Washington, DC: Federal Aviation Administration. Available: http://www.faa.gov/air_traffic/publications/cip/files/FY13-17/FY13-17_CIP_1_Intro_March_2012.pdf [May 2013].

FAA. (2011c). *Portfolio of Goals: FAA Performance Metrics—FY 2012*. Washington, DC: Federal Aviation Administration. Available: http://www.faa.gov/about/plans_reports/media/FY12_POG.pdf [May 2013].

FAA. (2012a). *FAA Notice 1100.332. Subject: Air Traffic Organization*. Effective Date: April 4, 2012. Available: http://www.faa.gov/documentLibrary/media/Notice/N%201100.332.pdf [May 2013].

FAA. (2012b). *JO 1030.7A. Air Traffic Organization Fatigue Risk Management*. Air Traffic Organization, Federal Aviation Administration, Washington, DC. Available: http://www.faa.gov/regulations_policies/orders_notices/index.cfm/go/document.information/documentID/1020290 [May 2013].

FAA. (2012c). *Administrator's Fact Book. June 2012*. Produced by the Deputy Assistant Administrator for Financial Services. Washington, DC: Federal Aviation Administration. Available: https://www.faa.gov/about/office_org/headquarters_offices/aba/admin_factbook [May 2013].

FAA. (2012d). *NextGen Implementation Plan: March 2012*. Washington, DC: Federal Aviation Administration. Available: http://www.faa.gov/nextgen/implementation/plan [May 2013].

FAA. (2012e). *VOR Minimum Operational Network (MON) Information Paper.* Available: http://www.faa.gov/about/office_org/headquarters_offices/ato/service_units/techops/navservices/gnss/mobileAll/VOR_MON.pdf [May 2013].

FAA. (2012f). *Aviation Safety 2012 Workforce Plan*. Washington, DC: Federal Aviation Administration. Available: http://www.faa.gov/about/office_org/headquarters_offices/agi/reports/media/faa%20aviation%20safety%20workforce%20plan%202012.pdf [May 2013].

FAA. (2012g). *WSSAS User's Guide, Revision 14, June 2012*. Available: ftp://ftp.volpe.dot.gov/pub/DTS-53/SSAS/ForKen/WSSAS_Users_Guide.pdf [February 2013].

GAO (Government Accountability Office). (2010). *Federal Aviation Administration: Agency Is Taking Steps to Plan for and Train Its Technician Workforce, but a More Strategic Approach Is Warranted*. GAO-11-91, October 22. Washington, DC: U.S. Government Printing Office. Available: http://www.gao.gov/assets/320/311691.pdf [May 2013].

GAO. (2012). *Next Generation Air Transport System: FAA Faces Implementation Challenges*. GAO-12-1011T, September 12. Washington, DC: U.S. Government Printing Office. Available: http://www.gao.gov/assets/650/648122.pdf [May 2013].

Grant Thornton. (2011). *Technical Operations Technician Staffing Model Assessment. Final Report.* Washington, DC: Federal Aviation Administration.

Grant Thornton. (2012). *Technical Operations Technician Staffing Model Recommendations Report Final.* Washington, DC: Federal Aviation Administration.

Hecht, M., and Handal, J. (2001). An analytical model for predicting the impact of maintenance resource allocation on air traffic control system availability. Pp. 1-7 in *Annual Reliability and Maintainability Symposium. 2001 Proceedings.* RM-066. Available: http://ieeexplore.ieee.org/xpl/login.jsp?tp=&arnumber=902440&url=http%3A%2F%2Fieeexplore.ieee.org%2Fiel5%2F7229%2F19492%2F00902440.pdf%3Farnumber%3D902440 [May 2013].

Hecht, M., Handal, J., Czekalski, L., and Rosin, A. (1998). Impact of maintenance staffing on availability of the U.S. air traffic control system. *Annual Reliability and Maintainability Symposium. 1998 Proceedings*. January 19-22, 1998, Beverly Hills, CA. Available: http://ieeexplore.ieee.org/xpl/login.jsp?tp=&arnumber=653669&url=http%3A%2F%2Fieeexplore.ieee.org%2Fstamp%2Fstamp.jsp%3Ftp%3D%26arnumber%3D653669 [May 2013].

Hecht, H.G., Handal, J., Goebel, M., and Demarco, F. (2000). An analytical model for predicting the impact of maintenance resource allocation on National Airspace System availability. *National Research Council Transportation Research Board 79th Annual Meeting*. Washington, DC. Available: http://www.reliability-safety-software.com/company/books.htm [May 2013].

Kahneman, D., Slovic, P., and Tversky, A., eds. (1982). *Judgment Under Uncertainty: Heuristics and Biases*. New York: Cambridge University Press.

Kohn, J.P., Friend, M.A., and Winterberger, C.A. (1996). *Fundamentals of Occupational Safety and Health*. Rockville, MD: Government Institutes.

Law, A., and Kelton, W.D. (2000). *Simulation Modeling and Analysis, Third Edition.* Boston: McGraw-Hill Higher Education.

Lehto, M., and Landry, S. (2013). *Introduction to Human Factors and Ergonomics for Engineers, Second Edition.* Taylor and Francis Group, LLC: Boca Raton, FL: CRC Press.

Moubray, J. (2001). *Reliability-centered Maintenance, Second Edition.* New York: Industrial Press, Inc.

NRC (National Research Council). (2006). *Staffing Standards for Aviation Safety Inspectors.* Washington, DC: The National Academies Press. Available: http://www.nap.edu/catalog.php?record_id=11742 [May 2013].

NRC. (2007). *Human-System Integration in the System Development Process: A New Look.* Washington, DC: The National Academies Press. Available: http://www.nap.edu/catalog.php?record_id=11893 [May 2013].

NRC. (2010). *TRB Special Report 301: Traffic Controller Staffing in the En Route Domain: A Review of the Federal Aviation Administration's Task Load Model.* Washington, DC: The National Academies Press. Available: http://www.nap.edu/catalog.php?record_id=13022 [May 2013].

Office of Management and Budget. (2003). *Circular No. A-76 Revised.* May 29. Available: http://www.whitehouse.gov/omb/circulars_a076_a76_incl_tech_correction [May 2013].

Office of Personnel Management. (2008). *End-to-End Hiring Initiative.* Available: http://archive.opm.gov/publications/endto-end-hiringinitiative.pdf [May 2013].

Office of Personnel Management. (undated). *OPM's Workforce Planning Model.* Available: http://www.opm.gov/policy-data-oversight/human-capital-management/reference-materials/strategic-alignment/workforceplanning.pdf [May 2013].

Ouvreloeil, T. (2001). The art of managing the backlog. *Maintenance Technology* February. Available: http://www.mt-online.com/february2001/the-art-of-managing-the-backlog [May 2013].

Professional Airways Systems Specialists. (2000). *Agreement Between the Professional Airways Systems Specialists Division, District No. 6—MEBA/NMU AFL-CIO and the Federal Aviation Administration. Effective July 2, 2000.* Available: https://apps3.opm.gov/portal/page/portal/LAIRS_Main/LAIRS_Document_Storage/E1992_02_10_X2005_02_09_1277_CA200067.pdf [May 2013].

Professional Aviation Safety Specialists. (2012). *Agreement Between the Professional Aviation Safety Specialists (AFL-CIO) and the Federal Aviation Administration, U.S. Department of Transportation. Effective December 16, 2012.* Available from http://www.passnational.org/homedocs/PASS_ATO_CBA.pdf [May 2013].

Rasmussen, J. 1983. Skills, rules, knowledge; signals, signs, and symbols, and other distinctions in human performance models. *IEEE Transactions on Systems, Man and Cybernetics* 13(3):257-266.

Roland, H.E., and Moriarty, B. (1990). *System Safety Engineering and Management, Second Edition.* New York: Wiley-Interscience.

Swallom, D., Lindberg, R., and Smith-Jackson, T. (2003). System safety principles and methods. Pp. 497-505 in *Handbook of Human Systems Integration.* H. Booher, ed. Hoboken, NJ: Wiley-Interscience.

U.S. Air Force. (1994). *Ground (Base) Radio Maintenance.* AFMS 38AC. July 1. Washington, DC: U.S. Air Force.

U.S. Air Force. (1995a). *Air Force Management Engineering Program (MEP) Processes.* Air Force Manual 38-208, Volume 1. March 31. Washington, DC: U.S. Air Force. Available: http://www.af.mil/shared/media/epubs/AFMAN38-208V1.pdf. [November 2012].

U.S. Air Force. (1995b). *Air Traffic Control and Landing Systems (ATCALS) Radar Maintenance.* AFMS 38AB. October 26. Washington, DC: U.S. Air Force.

U.S. Air Force. (1998). *Meteorological and Navigation Systems Equipment Maintenance Element.* AFMS 38AA. August 21. Washington, DC: U.S. Air Force.

U.S. Air Force. (2003). *Air Force Management Engineering Program (MEP) Quantification Tools. Air Force Manual 38-208, Volume 2.* HQ USAF/A1MR. November 19. Washington, DC: U.S. Air Force. Available: http://www.e-publishing.af.mil/shared/media/epubs/AFMAN38-208V2.pdf [November 2012].

U.S. Air Force. (2009). *U.S. Air Force Maintenance Metrics.* Maxwell AFB, Gunter Annex, AL: Air Force Logistics Management Agency. March 20. Available: http://www.aflma.hq.af.mil/shared/media/document/AFD-100107-055.pdf [May 2013].

U.S. Air Force. (2011). *Management of Manpower Requirements and Authorizations. Air Force Instruction 38-201.* September 26. AF/A1MR. Washington, DC: U.S. Air Force.

U.S. Air Force. (undated). *Air Force Human Systems Integration Handbook: Planning and Execution of Human Systems Integration.* Human Performance Optimization Division. 711 HPW/HPO. Brooks City-Base, TX: Directorate of Human Performance Integration. U.S. Air Force. Available: http://www.wpafb.af.mil/shared/media/document/AFD-090121-054.pdf [May 2013].

U.S. Government Printing Office. (2000). Executive Order 13180 of December 7, 2000. Air Traffic Performance-Based Organization. *Federal Register* 63(238) December 11:77493-77494. Available: http://www.gpo.gov/fdsys/pkg/FR-2000-12-11/pdf/00-31697.pdf [May 2013].

U.S. Government Printing Office. (2002). Executive Order 13264. Amendment to Executive Order 13180, Air Traffic Performance-Based Organization. June 4, 2002. *Federal Register Weekly Compilation of Presidential Documents* 38(23) June 10:963. Available: http://www.gpo.gov/fdsys/pkg/WCPD-2002-06-10/pdf/WCPD-2002-06-10-Pg963.pdf [May 2013].

U.S. Navy. (2000). *Navy Total Force Manpower Requirements Handbook*. Navy Manpower Analysis Center, Millington, TN. Available: http://www.public.navy.mil/bupers-npc/organization/navmac/manpowerprograms/Documents/ReqHdBk.pdf [May 2013].

U.S. Postal Service. (2011). *The Cost Structure of the Postal Service: Facts, Trends, and Policy Implications.* July 20. Risk Analysis Research Center. Report No. RARC-WP-11-007. Washington, DC: Office of the Inspector General, U.S. Postal Service. Available: https://www.uspsoig.gov/foia_files/rarc-wp-11-007.pdf [May 2013].

Wigfall, E.M. (2006). *How the National Performance Review Propelled the Federal Aviation Administration into a Performance Based Organization*. Northridge, CA: California State University.

Appendixes

Appendix A

Committee Biographies

Nancy T. Tippins (*Chair*) is senior vice president at Valtera, a division of the Corporate Executive Board. Her expertise includes the development and validation of selection tests and other forms of assessment for management and hourly employees and the design of performance management and leadership development programs. She has worked extensively with computer-based test administration, developing her first computer-administered test and test administration platform in 1991. Previously she worked in Fortune 100 companies developing and validating selection and assessment tools. She participated in the revision of the Principles for the Use and Validation of Personnel Selection Procedures and sits on committees to revise the Standards for Educational and Psychological Testing and the ISO 9000 standards for assessment. She is a member, fellow, and past president (2000-2001) of the Society for Industrial and Organizational Psychology, a fellow of the American Psychological Association, and a member of several private industry research groups. She has authored or co-authored articles on assessment and has served as associate editor for the *Scientist-Practitioner Forum of Personnel Psychology* and on the editorial board of the *Journal of Applied Psychology*. She has an M.S. and a Ph.D. in industrial and organizational psychology from the Georgia Institute of Technology.

Colin G. Drury is distinguished professor emeritus of industrial and systems engineering at University of Buffalo, State University of New York and president of Applied Ergonomics Group, Inc. Previously he was director of the Research Institute for Safety and Security in Transportation. His recent work focuses on the application of human factors techniques to inspection and maintenance processes, and he has published on industrial process control, quality control, aviation maintenance, security, and safety. He is a fellow of the Institute of Industrial Engineers, the Ergonomics Society, the International Ergonomics Association, and the Human Factors and Ergonomics Society. He received the Bartlett Medal of the Ergonomics Society and both the Fitts and Lauer Awards of the Human Factors Ergonomics Society. He received the Federal Aviation Administration's Excellence in Aviation Research Award (2005) and the American Association of Engineering Societies' Kenneth Andrew Roe Award (2006). He has an Honours B.Sc. in physics from the University of Sheffield, England, and a Ph.D. from the University of Birmingham, England, in engineering production specializing in ergonomics.

T. Mark Harrison (NAS) is distinguished professor of geochemistry in, and former chair of, the Department of Earth and Space Sciences at University of California, Los Angeles. His research areas include lithosphere tectonothermics, experimental and theoretical studies of magma transport, application of heat flow and diffusion theory to geological problems, development isotopic microanalysis, and planetary formation. He is a fellow of the Australian Academy of Sciences, American Geophysical Union, Geological Society of America, Geological Society of Australia, and the Geochemical Society. He has received the Presidential Young Investigator Award and the Day Medal of the Geological Society of America. He is a lifelong pilot and holds a commercial certificate with instrument and multi-engine ratings. He has a B.Sc. (Honors) from the University of British Columbia and a Ph.D. in earth sciences from the Australian National University.

Christopher Hart is vice chairman of the National Transportation Safety Board (NTSB). Previously he was a member of the NTSB, deputy director for Air Traffic Safety Oversight at the Federal Aviation Administration (FAA), and FAA assistant administrator for the Office of Safety, System Safety. He is a licensed pilot with commercial, multi-engine, and instrument ratings, as well as an attorney. He is a member of the District of Columbia Bar and the Lawyer-Pilots Bar Association. He has a B.S. and an M.S. in aerospace engineering from Princeton University and a J.D. from Harvard Law School.

Paul F. Hogan is senior vice president and practice director of Federal National Security and Emergency Preparedness at The Lewin Group. He applies microeconomics, econometrics, cost-benefit analyses, statistics, and operations research methods to problems of health economics, labor supply, compensation, training, performance, military staffing and readiness, and cost measurement. His research in health economics include workforce studies and measures of Medicare and Medicaid payment accuracy. He has a B.A. in economics from the University of Virginia and an M.S. in applied economics and finance from the University of Rochester.

Brian Norman is chief executive officer and founder of Compass Manpower Experts, LLC, and served recently as senior human resource advisor for the Changes for Justice Project, a U.S. Agency for International Development effort with the Attorney General's Office of the Republic of Indonesia. Previously, he served as commander of the Air Force Manpower Agency, directing efforts to determine manpower requirements, develop programming factors, manage Air Force performance management programs, execute competitive sourcing initiatives, and conduct special studies and analyses. Prior to that, he served as deputy director of plans and integration, deputy chief of staff for manpower and personnel, at Air Force Headquarters, where he guided strategic planning, visioning, and concepts of operation activities for Air Force manpower, personnel, and services. From 1995 through 2012, he served as a course director and adjunct professor at Ira P. Eaker College for Professional Development, Air University, Maxwell Air Force Base. He has a B.S. in industrial engineering from the University of Missouri, an M.S. in systems management from the University of Southern California, and an M.S. in strategic studies from Air University.

Tonya L. Smith-Jackson is professor and chair of industrial and systems engineering at North Carolina A&T State University. She is founder and director of the Assessment and Cognitive Ergonomics Lab and co-director of the Safety Engineering and Human-Computer Interaction Labs. She is a member of the American Society of Safety Engineers, the Human Factors and Ergonomics Society, the Institute of Industrial Engineers, the Association for Psychological Science, and the Society of Women Engineers. She is certified by the Board of Certification in Professional Ergonomics. Her work has focused on research, teaching, and service efforts to ensure processes and technologies are equitable and inclusive across cultures, genders, abilities, and generations. Her research has been funded by the National Science Foundation, National Institute for Occupational Safety and Health, Army Research Office, United Parcel Service, Toshiba Corporation of Japan, Carilion Clinic, and Carilion Biomedical Institute. She has a B.A. in psychology from the University of North Carolina at Chapel Hill and an M.S. and a Ph.D. in psychology/ergonomics from North Carolina State University.

William J. Strickland is president and chief executive officer of the Human Resources Research Organization (HumRRO) in Alexandria, Virginia. Previously, he was a HumRRO vice president directing its Workforce Analysis and Training Systems Division. Before that, he served 26 years in the U.S. Air Force and retired as a colonel. He is a fellow of the American Psychological Association (APA), a past president of its Division of Military Psychology, and the Division's representative on APA's Council of Representatives. He currently serves on APA's Policy and Planning Board and as a member-at-large on the APA Board of Directors. He is a graduate of the U.S. Air Force Academy and holds a Ph.D. in industrial and organizational psychology from Ohio State University.

Elmore M. Wigfall is a retired 36-year veteran of the Federal Aviation Administration (FAA) and an adjunct instructor in the Department of Electronic Technology at Antelope Valley Community College, Lancaster, California. His FAA experience was in air traffic control technical operations, and he has held positions ranging from Air Traffic Systems Specialist (electronics technician) to Systems Management Office, Manager. He has more than 3,000 hours of FAA technical, management, and leadership training and has completed more than 150 hours of training in mediation and conflict resolution with practical application and experience conducting mediations in civil court cases. Currently, he volunteers with the California Academy of Mediation Professionals as a civil dispute mediator for small claims, limited jurisdiction, and civil harassment cases in the Los Angeles Superior Court System. He has a B.S. in Computer Science from the University of Central Oklahoma and an M.P.A. from California State University, Northridge.

Appendix B

Open Session Speakers

MEETING 1

October 18-19, 2012
Washington, DC

10:00 a.m. **Public Welcome & Study Introduction**
Barbara Wanchisen, Director, Board on Human-Systems Integration

10:30 a.m. **Sponsor Perspective**
Charge and Expectations of the Study
2012 Airway Transportation Systems Specialists (ATSS) Briefing for the National Academy of Sciences0
Rich McCormick, Labor Analysis, ALA-1, Federal Aviation Administration (FAA)
Vaughn Turner, Vice President of Technical Operations Service Unit, FAA
Gene Crabtree, Deputy Vice President of Technical Operations Service Unit, FAA
James Thomas, Program Manager, Technical Operations Workforce, FAA
Kevin Brathwaite, Consultant, Grant Thornton

MEETING 2

December 6-7, 2012
Washington, DC

8:30 a.m. **FAA Briefing—Integrated Control Facilities**

Future Facilities Program Overview
Austin Aurandt, Acting Manager, Program Management Team, Air Traffic Control Facilities Directorate, AJW-2, FAA

9:30 a.m.	**FAA Discussion** Gene Crabtree, Deputy Vice President of Technical Operations Service Unit, FAA
10:30 a.m.	**Break**
10:45 a.m.	**Air Traffic Control Staffing—U.S. Air Force Manpower Directorate** Kent B. White, Colonel, U.S. Air Force, Air Force Personnel Center, Director of Manpower Dennis Carter, Chief of Management Engineering, Manpower Directorate
Noon	**Lunch with Continued Discussion with Attendees** Nancy Tippins, Chair
1:00 p.m.	**Professional Aviation Safety Specialists (PASS) Presentation and Discussion** Mike Perrone, National President, PASS, American Federation of Labor-Congress of Industrial Organizations (AFL-CIO) Rich Casey, National Vice President, PASS, AFL-CIO
3:00 p.m.	**Break**
3:15 p.m.	**FAA NextGen Presentations** **Next Generation Air Traffic Management System** Steve Bradford, Chief Scientist-Architecture & NextGen Development, FAA **NextGen and Technical Operations** Barbara Fisher, Manager for the National Airspace System Implementation Harmonization Division, ANG-D3, FAA

MEETING 3

January 23-24, 2013
Washington, DC

10:15 a.m.	**FAA Question and Answer Session** Nancy Tippins, Chair

MEETING 4

February 27-28, 2013
Irvine, CA

Report Writing Meeting